Update
Hong Kong

Other titles in this series:

Update Hong Kong

Martin F. Bennett

Alison R. Lanier was the originator of the Update series and is currently editor of *The International American,* a monthly newsletter for Americans living and working abroad.

Intercultural Press, Inc.
Yarmouth, Maine

Library of Congress Catalog No. 92-9174

ISBN 1-877864-02-1

Published by Intercultural Press, Inc.

Cover design by Letter Space

Printed in the United States of America

For information, address:

Intercultural Press, Inc.
P.O. Box 700
Yarmouth, ME 04096

Update
Hong Kong

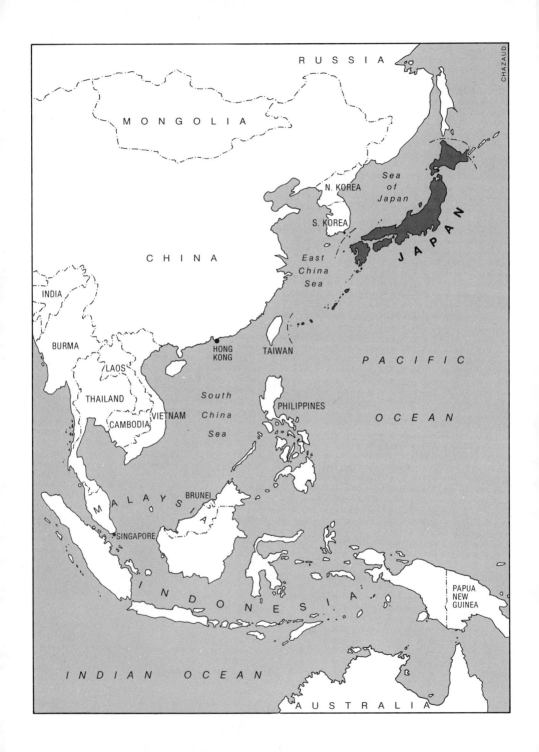

RUSSIA

MONGOLIA

CHINA

N. KOREA

S. KOREA

Sea of Japan

JAPAN

East China Sea

INDIA

BURMA

HONG KONG

TAIWAN

LAOS

THAILAND

PACIFIC OCEAN

VIETNAM

CAMBODIA

South China Sea

PHILIPPINES

MALAYSIA

BRUNEI

SINGAPORE

INDONESIA

PAPUA NEW GUINEA

INDIAN OCEAN

AUSTRALIA

CHAZAUD

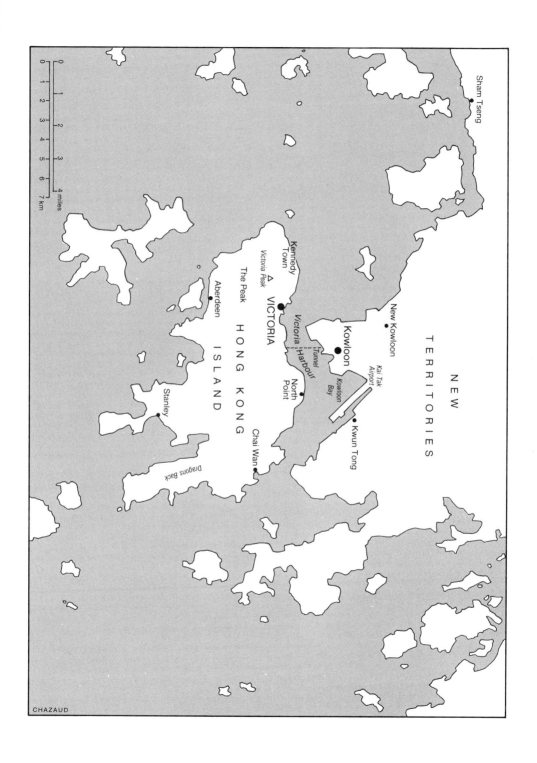

Sham Tseng

Kennedy
Town

Victoria Peak

The Peak

Aberdeen

△ VICTORIA

HONG KONG

New Kowloon

Kowloon

Victoria Harbour
Tunnel

ISLAND

North
Point

Kowloon
Bay

Kai Tak
Airport

Stanley

Chai Wan

Dragons Back

Kwun Tong

NEW

TERRITORIES

0 1 2 3 4 5 6 7 km
0 1 2 3 4 miles

CHAZAUD

TABLE OF CONTENTS

1

ßackground

A HISTORICAL VIEW OF HONG KONG AND CHINA

Hong Kong, People's Republic of China—1997! Hong Kong's new nomenclature will highlight this former British territory's sensitive position in the current evolution of China and its relationship with the West. While you are living or conducting business in Hong Kong, your personal and professional life will be significantly affected by the sociohistorical patterns of this nation and by the manner in which China and Britain prepare this world-class city-state for its entry into the twenty-first century.

To be a Hong Kong "belonger" in the 1990s, you must grasp the historical context that has framed this Asian city of 5.8 million people and linked its destiny with China's. Hong Kong's history can be divided into five major phases: imperial, colonial, post-World War II or indigenization, global, and assimilation. Each of these historical periods has left its imprint on the development of Hong Kong.

The Imperial Phase

Hong Kong's first inhabitants arrived in approximately 3000 B.C., seafarers whose stone artifacts are periodically discovered on Hong Kong Island. Ironically, these were Hong Kong's first boat people,

1

members of Yueh tribes who successfully navigated northward from Southeast Asia. These ancient wanderers eventually settled into a life of fishing and farming.

Centuries later, in 221 B.C., when China was unified under the Han Dynasty, the city of Guangzhou (Canton) came under Chinese control. From this seaport, located ninety miles from the mouth of the Zhujiang (Pearl) River, the Cantonese established extensive trade routes. Outsiders also came: Roman traders visited Guangzhou in about 138 B.C., and centuries later, in A.D. 758, seafaring Arabs burned the city. Seeking to maintain its authority, the Eastern Han Dynasty (A.D. 25-270) extended its control from Central China into the southern and coastal areas of China, posting infantrymen in Kowloon. The tomb at Lei Cheung Uk is witness to this early unification of the lands of Hong Kong with the authority of centralized China. In A.D. 936 additional Chinese soldiers were stationed in the New Territories (areas around the mouth of the Pearl River) to protect the pearl industry.

Between 960 and 1279 Chinese migrants, continuing to travel southward, established themselves in the northern areas of Hong Kong, creating walled cities and rice fields. Their architectural remains are scattered throughout the New Territories as are their descendants, who proudly bear the names of Tang, Hau, Pang, Lio, and Man and who represent the most indigenous of all the current Hong Kong peoples. The dome-shaped lime kilns scattered about Hong Kong's coastal areas date to this era. Lime was a valued commodity during this period since it was used to waterproof and caulk boats as well as to fortify the soil for crops. From the thirteenth to the fifteenth centuries, ship traffic supporting the entrepreneurial instincts of the Cantonese increased. Temples, such as those at Joss House Bay and Castle Peak Bay, were constructed and were regularly visited by Cantonese seafaring worshipers praying for safe voyages.

In response to the Manchu invasion, the vanquished aristocracy of the last Sung Dynasty of the twelfth century established its last court on Lantau Island in Hong Kong after fleeing the chaos of dynastic upheaval in central China. The Ching Dynasty period fort at Tung Lung again recalls Beijing's expansionism and its military control over the territories surrounding the coastal areas, which during the colonial period would come to be known as Hong Kong. (It was not until the late 1800s, however, that the name Hong Kong first appeared on the official maps of China.)

The Colonial Phase

Colonial Hong Kong is an extension of Guangzhou's development as a major Chinese port and the tragic conflicts over the regulation of trade with the Western colonial powers. During the sixteenth century the Pearl River basin shifted from a peasant to a semifeudal or semicolonial economy. Early Portuguese explorers established a significant dialogue with China, which in 1557 earned them the privilege of organizing a colonial presence in Macao, at the mouth of the Pearl River. Although British ships were anchored in the Pearl River as early as 1637, it was not until 1715 that the British East Indies Company properly established itself in Guangzhou. China struggled to reconcile its suspicion of Western traders and its interest in the products westerners introduced to Chinese society. In an effort to control the relationship, the Chinese initiated the "Eight Restrictions," which dictated the terms of trade with westerners.

An additional tension existed in China during this period, one which occurs cyclically throughout Chinese history. Agrarian-based northern and central China largely prohibited external trade, with hierarchical and authoritarian control exercised according to Confucian ethic. The coastal cities and provinces, such as Guangzhou, however, were entrepreneurial and less receptive to centralized control. There was an adventuresome streak among the people of the coastal cities. Trading was not as predictable as the agricultural life. The whims of sea and wind and the gun-laden trading ships of the European and American powers made it chancy. Far distant from the center of imperial power in Beijing, the freewheeling, mobile, and entrepreneurial Cantonese of Guangzhou traded with southern Asia.

China formalized its interest in southern China when Emperor Qian Ling mandated Guangzhou as China's sole port for the rapidly expanding Sino-Western trade and established the Canton merchant's guild, the "Co-Hong." In the nineteenth century, opium from British-controlled India became the commodity that fueled the Sino-British balance of trade. The three-way exchange of opium, silver, and Chinese products, while creating greater financial solvency for the financially weakened economy of India, seriously undermined the social and moral character of China. By 1832 Britain was smuggling 23,570 chests of opium, each containing between 130 and 160 pounds, into Imperial China despite the official ban on its importation. Not only did this lethal drug become a corrupting force within the social structure of China, it also created an arena for graft and corruption within the imperial bureaucracy, which in turn became a source of excessive profits for both the Chinese and the "foreign devils." Two wars were eventually fought over the control of opium and Western trade, the Anglo-Chinese war of 1840-1842 and the Anglo-Chinese war of 1856-1858 (popularly known as the Opium Wars to North American historians and as the Arrow Wars to British historians). The treaties which ended these wars gave the British the island of Hong Kong in 1842 (Treaty of Nanking) and Kowloon and Stonecutter Island in 1860 (Convention of Peking). In 1898 Hong Kong's borders were extended to include the New Territories, thus adding 370 square miles to its boundaries. These treaties shattered China's ethnocentric stance vis-a-vis the rest of the world and forced it to set up a grudging dialogue with the West. Hong Kong became the site of a more or less permanent British presence in China and a convenient transshipment base for Sino-Western trade. Until the advent of the Chinese Revolution and World War II, Hong Kong continued its role as an Asian colony of a great Western power. The British securely established themselves by combining the entrepreneurial instincts of Chinese culture with Western laissez-faire autocracy based on English jurisprudence. The restored Repulse Bay Hotel and Flagstaff House recall this period of *taipans* and *compradores,* colonial administrators and militia, expatriates and questionable adventurers who all bartered and traded in this Victorian enclave. They built their own homes, university, primary and secondary schools, churches, and synagogue. They also built military forts to house the British nationals and their Gurkha colleagues, infantrymen recruited from the hillsides of Nepal in the service of the Crown, who were renowned for their bravery. From this secure vantage point, the British and the Hong Kong Chinese witnessed the demise of Imperial China and the birth of the People's Republic of China (PRC), continuing all the while to quietly grow and flourish (from 3,650 people on land and 2,000 fishermen on boats in its founding years to 530,000 residents in 1916 and then to one million in 1937).

The Indigenization Phase

Under traditional British territorial administration Hong Kong prospered. Its Chinese and Western populations developed economically, yet the political and social climate of Hong Kong always reflected the political, social, and economic reorganizations of "The Mainland." The Chinese Revolution of 1911, overthrowing the dynastic control of the Manchus, caused major immigration into Hong Kong. The antiforeign attitudes that developed in China in the 1920s were manifested in Hong Kong by the general strikes of 1925-26. In response to the aggression of Japan and its "21 demands," thousands of Chinese nationals fled China to secure a "safe harbor" in Hong Kong. The momentous events within China and Asia during the 1940s and 1950s challenged the character of colonial Hong Kong and forced the government to address the rising social needs of its indigenous peoples. As a result of the Sino-Japanese War (1937-1945), 750,000 refugees fled to Hong Kong only to face Japanese occupation. Hong Kong's burgeoning economy was stalled as the occupied colony struggled to feed its people. By the end of the occupation in 1945, Hong Kong's population had dwindled to six hundred thousand people, and concern mounted that Hong Kong would be returned to the mainland as a consequence of World War II. However, the British maintained control.

When the People's Republic of China was established in 1949, Hong Kong again faced a major influx of refugees, numbering approximately 750,000, and a major economic restructuring. Due to Britain's participation in the United Nation's embargo on trade with the PRC, Hong Kong's profitable China trade was restricted, forcing it to shift from being a transshipment center for Chinese goods into becoming a manufacturing center as China's refugee business community brought not only its funds and business acumen but sometimes whole factories to be reconstructed in Hong Kong. The colony established itself as a world center for plastics, fabrics, and apparel manufacturing.

Although Hong Kong weathered several onslaughts of refugees, it wasn't until the Christmas Day fire of 1953 in Shek Kip Mei that its social structure was severely challenged. Overnight, the colonial government faced the need to house 53,000 homeless people. Prior to the fire, arriving refugees had built their own homes in random fashion on Hong Kong's hillsides. These sites were overcrowded and lacked proper utilities and sanitation. The disaster required action and the government responded with an aggressive housing program, providing homes in public subsidized units for close to 50 percent of its people. However, the influence of conservative elements within the government has continued to limit the social-service infrastructure to reacting to major crises rather than establishing a comprehensive social-service policy as is often seen in the United States and Western Europe.

In summary, during the indigenization phase the central government became stronger as it responded more to the needs of its people and began to represent their interests not only in England but also throughout the world. The government became less a colonial administration at the service of the Crown and began to assert itself as a functioning government with strong ties to England, yet representing the interests of its indigenous peoples.

The Global Phase

During the 1960s, 1970s, and 1980s Hong Kong developed a unique identity in the global market. Although still under the administrative influence and direction of the United Kingdom, it developed into a major world force in its own right, representing Chinese and international interests. As globalized markets expanded, Hong Kong was clearly no longer just a colonial transshipment point or a vibrant Asian manufacturing center of relatively cheap and unsophisticated products. It had become a strategic center for global sourcing and marketing, with a special potential for an emerging trade with the People's Republic of China and Southeast Asia. During the mid-1960s, Hong Kong yet again reacted to the upheavals of China's ideological battles. While most of China suffered under the destructive rise of the Red Guard during the Cultural Revolution, Hong Kong observed minor violence in the form of demonstrations, fights, and some bombings. Ultimately, those reactions were controlled by the pro-China factions in Hong Kong since economic and political destabilization in Hong Kong was not supportive to the best interests of China. The PRC, noting the dynamic importance of Hong Kong, slowly and quietly developed a political and economic presence there.

In the 1970s, in response to growing protectionist attitudes around the world, Hong Kong industries had to become more technologically innovative and had to upgrade their product quality and production efficiency. In addition, the emergence of the newly industrialized countries (NICs) of Southeast Asia and their relatively cheaper labor costs drew financial and business interests away from Hong Kong. This shift, which initially caused some concern in the Hong Kong political and economic communities, was offset in the 1980s by the increasing investment from the PRC. By the end of the decade, 40 percent of the PRC's foreign exchange was earned in Hong Kong. Over three hundred PRC-related companies were set up in the territory, and 20 percent of all bank deposits were institutionally controlled by Beijing. Equally important, Hong Kong interests accounted for 60 percent of all investment in China, and over 60 percent of China's joint ventures with international partners involved a Hong Kong business. Currently, Hong Kong companies employ 1.5 to 2 million people in China. Hong Kong was becoming the financial midwife for global trade with China, confirmed by the increased investments of the United States, Canada, Europe, and Japan within the territory. A stable currency and a secure government with a proven history of limited intervention made Hong Kong during the 1980s the most stable and thoroughly laissez-faire of all business centers in Asia, including Singapore, Taiwan, and Japan.

As the 1997 transition approaches, however, Hong Kong is once again redefining itself. Fearing the potential limitations of the takeover, the major "Hongs" or trading companies have developed globalized strategies. For example, Jardine, Matherson and Co. moved its headquarters to Bermuda, and seventy Hong Kong-based holding companies have relocated worldwide. The Hong Kong Shanghai Bank, while maintaining its main operations in Hong Kong, has shifted approximately 72 percent of its assets outside of the territory to a holding company in the United Kingdom, although it still makes 80 percent of its profit from Hong Kong. In addition 25 percent of all companies listed on the Hang Seng, the Hong Kong Stock Exchange, have moved their corporate headquarters out of Hong Kong. This outward trend, however, is seemingly being balanced by an influx of international money invested in the Hong Kong economy by Western and Asian interests, with Japan leading the way. Thus, a global balancing game has developed that seeks a point of equilibrium between multinational financial interests and the expanding interests of the People's Republic of China. Strategically, Hong Kong has developed a modern container port (a shipping port specially equipped to handle containerized cargo), which is now second only to Rotterdam; a rapid transit system; a major urban relocation program, creating "New Towns" to house and provide work for the emerging young generation; and a new airport with its own rail system to accommodate the air traffic of the twenty-first century.

The Assimilation Phase

The original treaties that ceded the New Territories to Britain were of limited duration and questionable legality and are due to expire July 1, 1997. It would be impossible, morally or militarily, for the British to support their claim of full sovereignty over Hong Kong Island and a small section of Kowloon east of Boundary Street. Thus, in just a few short years, the control of Hong Kong will pass to the PRC. Hong Kong has long been a community where people came to find a livelihood and the resources to prosper, and it has continually integrated newcomers. The 1997 transition is a remarkable political and sociological phenomenon. Hong Kong's nonviolent assimilation into China appears to counter the trend of the 1990s toward decentralization of political control and the factioning of nations into ethnic and cultural groups as witnessed by Eastern Europe. While many scholars will identify Chinese people as one cultural group, Hong Kong Chinese are clearly a culture to themselves. Over 50 percent of Hong Kong residents were born and educated in the laissez-faire, pseudo-democratic and entrepreneurial atmosphere of Hong Kong, clearly demarcating them as culturally distinct from their mainland cousins. Now, however, with 1997 around the corner, the stage is set for the massive assimilation of Hong Kong's 5.8 million people into the political and economic structure of the PRC, which has announced that Hong Kong will become part of "one China" with "two systems."

Any expatriate stationed in Hong Kong during these assimilation years of the 1990s will witness a remarkable political transition as China, the United Kingdom, and the indigenous Hong Kong Chinese go about restructuring Hong Kong to fit the one China/two systems concept. It will be the first time in history that a major capitalistic center will peacefully integrate itself into the workings of a state espousing socialism and communism. Hong Kong's future role is critical to China because no other Chinese city has its global infrastructure or economic standing. However, the still unanswered question is this: "Will Hong Kong maintain its worldwide position after 1997?" The images of the violent and repressive actions of the leadership of China toward the students demonstrating in Tienanmen Square in June, 1989, must be juxtaposed with the one million Hong Kong students and young adults who marched in Hong Kong in open opposition to such unacceptable tactics. China's response was the inclusion of a nonsubversive rule into the Basic Law to address any demonstration that might occur after 1997.

Open criticism has been directed at the British government for its failure to establish a more democratic government in Hong Kong which would survive in 1997. It was only in September, 1991, that Hong Kong had its first election for seats on the Legislative Council. Currently 1 percent of Hong Kong's population, approximately 62,000 persons, have emigrated to other countries. More alarming is the fact that this group represents 10 percent of the highly skilled middle class.

The Lessons from History

What then are the lessons from history that an expatriate taking up residency in Hong Kong in the 1990s should consider?

1. Hong Kong, although known in many parts of the world as the product of Western colonial expansion, is essentially a Chinese city—geographically, culturally, and historically, and it has always reacted to the pulse of the mainland.

2. Not all legacies of Western colonial presence have been exploitative and culturally destructive. Without the financial and administrative policy of the United Kingdom, Hong Kong would not have developed as it has and, consequently, would not be in the strategic position to assist Western and Asian interests in China and China's interest in global markets.

3. The current expansion of Chinese control over the territory is but another manifestation of China's cyclical exercising and relaxing of authority over its coastal areas. In recent years, China has become increasingly aware of the economic importance of relating with the world community and the entrepreneurial Hong Kong Chinese who will be the leaders in the dialogue.

4. China has always been attracted to Hong Kong, allowing it the luxury of maintaining contact with and observing Western and capitalistic ways yet also keeping enough distance to evaluate their appropriateness for the development of China.

5. The indigenous peoples of Hong Kong, predominantly the Cantonese, are remarkably resilient and creative. They have been able to adjust economic variables to maintain employment and to remain externally competitive in worldwide markets. From the 1 percent who leave each year, the world will receive valuable resources. Those who remain will find a way to utilize the political and economic infrastructure of Hong Kong, China, and thrive.

WHAT HONG KONG IS LIKE

Introduction by Air

With few exceptions, your first glimpse of Hong Kong ("The Fragrant Harbor" in Chinese) will be from a plane as you approach Kai Tak (Hong Kong International) Airport, one of the busiest airports in the world. Its tarmac, originally built by the Japanese in World War II, juts out 3,390 meters (a mile and a half) directly into the harbor on mostly reclaimed land. The two approaches to the runway are also unique: from one direction the descent is over the Kowloon Peninsula, giving the traveler an extended view of the island; from the other, the approach is over sporadic islands and unpopulated coastal areas until the very last moment. From either direction, you won't want to miss the landing.

Departing from the airport, you will immediately be struck by the atmosphere of a truly Chinese city. The sounds, smells, and activities are clearly those of a highly urbanized Chinese center. You will also be struck by the many contrasts—some of them immediately apparent, some more subtle and more difficult to pinpoint. There is, of course, the twentieth-century Hong Kong of postcard fame, with its world-class hotels and shopping centers. There are also narrow, crowded streets, balconies with colorful splashes of flowers and fluttering laundry, and factories jammed into small buildings.

Hong Kong Island, Kowloon, and the New Territories

Traditionally, Hong Kong has been grouped into three major sections: Hong Kong Island, Kowloon, and the New Territories, with its 235 outlying islands. Hong Kong Island is approximately 77.5 square kilometers (twenty-nine square miles), and has traditionally been the political and economic center of the territory, housing most government and financial offices as well as shopping centers. It has also been the major residential location for expatriates. Hong Kong Island, crowned by Victoria Peak, is known for its Central District (commercial area of offices, shops, and hotels); its Wanchai and Causeway Bay area (night life, cultural area, and yacht harbor); and the Southern District—Aberdeen Harbor (boat harbor and seafood restaurants), Repulse Bay (beach and restaurants), and Stanley (beach, American Country Club, and street markets).

Kowloon occupies approximately 12 square kilometers (4.3 square miles) of a small peninsula on the mainland. Formerly a residential and industrial center, Kowloon is now developing as a burgeoning tourist and recreation center. The tip of the peninsula, Tsim Sha Tsui, is known for its grand hotels, shops on Nathan Road, and now the new Cultural Center and Space Museum. It has also become an attractive residential area for many singles or expatriate couples because of its accessibility to transportation and leisure activities.

The New Territories, approximately 980.5 square kilometers (370 square miles), consists of the landmass between Kowloon and the border of the PRC and the 235 surrounding islands. Approximately 2.2 million people live in this section. The territory offers a change of environmental pace, with its rice paddies, duck and fish farms, flower and vegetable plots, and many small Buddhist monasteries tucked in the remote hills of the "dragon's back." With the increased number of government-sponsored housing schemes, the New Territories has become a prime location for economic expansion and urban relocation. Many of the 235 islands are uninhabited. The largest, Lantau, is three times larger than Hong Kong Island itself and is the site of a "Western-style" planned community, multiple resort and beach clubs, and a new airport. Some islands are primarily oriented toward fishing while others are used by the government for a variety of purposes: a munitions storage area, a detention camp for boat people in transit to other countries or repatriation to Vietnam, and a correctional institution, among others.

Housing

Few countries, or even major international cities, can claim that they have provided public housing for more than half of their population.

Hong Kong can make this claim because of its commitment to public rental and subsidized accommodations as well as to new home-ownership programs. Currently, approximately 2.8 million people are housed in rental estates and courts, and 120,500 people reside in temporary housing areas. In addition to these services, the Hong Kong Housing Society manages seventeen rental estates, providing another source of low-rental homes. It is estimated that in the early 1990s Hong Kong will provide housing for approximately 57 percent of its population.

The impetus for these programs was, as mentioned earlier, the Shek Kip Mei squatter fire, which left 53,000 people homeless on Christmas Day 1953. In less than two months, the Public Works Department had provided emergency housing for 35,000 people, followed in 1954 with the famous "seven-story mountains," the H-shaped, seven-story resettlement blocks which are scattered through-out the territory. Today's estates are considerably larger, soaring to thirty-six stories. Each year fifty thousand flats are built, 25 percent of these units being offered for sale. Each of these extensive housing developments has its own commercial center for shops, banks, restaurants, clinics, and a market; a hostel for elders; nurseries, kindergartens, primary and secondary schools; gardens and play areas; a car park; and a terminus for buses and minibuses.

A distinctive feature of Hong Kong's current housing policy is the development of "New Towns." Although urban development sites are still available on Hong Kong Island and in Kowloon, in 1972 the government began to lay plans for the development of the open areas of the New Territories to produce new towns which would include not only private housing and recreational opportunities but also commercial properties. This highly successful program has lowered the population density in the more congested areas of Hong Kong and thus increased the quality of life. It has also proven to be a wise economic investment as the New Towns are developing into thriving business and recreation centers in their own right. By the mid-1990s, approximately three million people will live in the New Towns.

Social Services

The quality and extent of social services varies. A noncontributive social security system provides public assistance programs, a special needs allowance, criminal justice and law enforcement, compensation for injuries, assistance for traffic accident victims, and emergency relief. Family welfare services help families and individuals solve relational and adjustment problems through fifty-four family service centers. Child welfare provides temporary care for orphans, abandoned children, or wanderers. There is an extensive youth program as well as institutional and community-care services for the elderly.

Environmental Protection

Pollution continues to be a major concern in Hong Kong. Its causes are numerous: vehicle emissions, noise pollution from pile driving and building, indiscriminate dumping of toxic materials, water pollution from the stationary water in the typhoon shelters and *nullahs* (storm drainage ditches), and the pollution of streams in the New Territories by livestock and chemical wastes. The latter has devastated fishing in Tolo Harbor and ruined the summer oysters with high levels of cadmium and lead. It is not unusual for several beaches to be closed during the summer months because of high bacteria counts in the water. The rapid industrial growth of the 1970s and 1980s, with little environmental control or consciousness, has created an increasing ecological hazard. The Environmental Protection Department has recently concluded that half of the factories in major industrial areas have inappropriate disposal procedures for their waste. Throughout the 1980s a number of legislative measures were enacted to control air pollution, waste disposal, and road traffic. Increased staff, money, and power has given the Environmental Protection Department the muscle to carry out the much needed reform. Unfortunately, many people don't demonstrate concern for their environment; thus, the government must not only fight the pollution itself but also mount media campaigns aimed at heightening consciousness of the problem.

Crime and Drugs

Hong Kong, like so many major urban areas, is struggling with drug-trafficking problems. It is estimated that 8 percent of the population eleven years old and over are addicts. An increasing volume of drug business has produced stepped-up police efforts at control and seizure. Heroin is relatively cheap and is considered to be the drug of choice. Imported from the "golden triangle" (Burma, Laos, and Thailand), the drug passes from Burma through China's western Yunnan Province and is smuggled into Hong Kong either by junk at night or through crowded border crossings. Marijuana and hashish are difficult to obtain and are expensive. The government has responded to drug problems with a comprehensive program of education, treatment, rehabilitation, and law enforcement.

Organized crime in Hong Kong originated among the historic Triad societies, whose purpose was to prevent the erosion of Manchu power. The government has attempted to crack down on the drug lords with tougher laws governing illegal gambling and drug abuse and is imposing stricter penalties. Today these crime syndicates, frequently with worldwide affiliates in the Chinese communities of the United States and the United Kingdom, control prostitution, drug trafficking and extortion throughout the territory. Hong Kong has been experiencing an increase in robberies and Triad gang fights. There has been a 40 percent increase in the use of firearms even though guns are outlawed in Hong Kong and, traditionally, the weapon of choice has been the chopping cleaver.

There is a significant smuggling operation between Hong Kong and China. Fishermen have cast away their nets for the nefarious life of smuggling electrical goods, alcohol, and cigarettes. They have now expanded their product line to include stolen cars and motorbikes. The growing number of armed robberies in Hong Kong is attributed to the increasing importation of contraband firearms, which are illegal in Hong Kong except for official purposes.

The Hong Kong police force is also facing a significant transition. Many of the best officers have emigrated. The government is attempting to address the issue with additional pay increases to maintain and motivate the officers, clearly remembering the unfortunate past when prominent members of the force succumbed to corruption and bribes. Actually, when put into perspective, Hong Kong may not be very different from other major international cities regarding general street crime. However, most expatriates consider Hong Kong to be a relatively safe city, since they rarely find themselves in dangerous situations. The worst event that may befall visitors is a picked pocket in a crowded subway or while shopping in a crowded market.

THE GOVERNMENT

Pre-1997

Hong Kong's current government mirrors the traditional British colonial structure. The governor is appointed by the queen and holds office for an unspecified period of time "according to her pleasure." As titular commander-in-chief and chief administrator, he presides over the Executive Council and the Legislative Council. The function of the Executive Council is to advise the governor on his decisions. The Legislative Council's prime constitutional functions are to legislate, to control public expenditures, and to monitor the performance of the administration. While the formal powers of the governor appear far-reaching, in practice this system provides stability and balance. The councils are made up of ex officio and appointed members. Hong Kong has no tradition of elected representation other than elections for the Urban Council, whose functions are related to the provision of cultural and recreational services in Hong Kong. Currently, some members of the Legislative Council are chosen by popular election, but the concept of accountability to one's constituents does not exist.

The Judiciary consists of the Supreme Court, the District Court, the Magistrate's Court, the Coroner's Court, the Juvenile Court, and also the Lands Tribunal, the Labor Tribunal, and the Small Claims Tribunal. Hong Kong does have a jury system for serious criminal offenses, and expatriates may be required to serve. You may wish to familiarize yourself with English common law and the law of equity. Statutory law is created by way of ordinances, and the ordinances generally follow the principles of English Acts of Parliament.

Post-1997

The Sino-British Agreement of December 19, 1984, briefly stated, maintains that the United Kingdom will continue to administer Hong Kong up to June 30, 1997; after that date the PRC will govern Hong Kong under the concept of one country/two systems. Hong Kong will become a Special Administrative Region (SAR) of the PRC, retaining much of its autonomy and familiar capitalistic life-style.

The greatest political challenge facing Hong Kong in the 1990s is the implementation of the Sino-British Declaration of 1984. To accomplish this task, the National People's Congress set up the Basic Law Drafting Committee, whose job it was to write up the Basic Law document. The Basic Law Consultative Committee, composed of many influential business members, was assigned the job of collecting the views of Hong Kong people and presenting them to the Basic Law Drafting Committee. In February 1990 the Committee completed the arduous task of drafting the Basic Law and submitted it to the National People's Congress in April of that year. Throughout the process there was concern about the ability of the People's Republic of China representatives, the British government, and business leaders of Hong Kong to effectively represent the interests of the Hong Kong people. Having accomplished this task, the question still remains as to whether the People's Republic of China will guarantee the rights outlined for Hong Kong people. The current rise of political parties seeking elected positions on the Legislative Council seems to have captured the interest of the young professionals of Hong Kong and their desire to be proactive in maintaining democratic traditions in Hong Kong.

While many Hong Kong people prefer the stability of the British-supported political system to the frequently erratic and unpredictable nature of the Chinese system, few have the power or position to influence the future. The Agreement of 1984 was constructed with minimal input from the people of Hong Kong, a crucial point in understanding the current atmosphere in Hong Kong. The British originally established a benevolent oligarchy for their colony, which, of course, did nothing to encourage democracy. While attempts have since been made to democratize Hong Kong by increased participation through district elections and elections of Legislative Council members, the electorate's response has been minimal. The overall feeling in Hong Kong is that of an apolitical population, a point of continual criticism. Hong Kong people simply identify with their family and their kinship network, not with a regional or political entity. Nor does the PRC want to encourage politicization in Hong Kong. China may be able to tolerate a capitalistic economic system as part of its one China/two systems approach, but it is not ready to have a democratic *political* system of close to six million Chinese people sitting on its southern coast. The current agreement and transfer of power seem to meet the interests of the two megapowers—China and Great Britain. Because of PRC investments, Hong Kong in many ways is already part of China. Massive infusions of Chinese capital continue to flow into Hong Kong and the adjacent Guangdong Province. Current shifts of light manufacturing into China to support the development of the provinces and its economic zones enhances Hong Kong's role as one of the PRC's premier economic centers.

Although most citizens of Hong Kong are not directly involved in the reunification process, it is certainly on everyone's mind, mostly in the form of the question: "Will my family and my family's future prosper economically, socially, educationally, and culturally under the administration of the People's Republic of China as it has under the British colonial government?" To understand this concern it is important to remember that the majority of the current population were born in Hong Kong and the remainder were primarily agrarian refugees from a chaotic China. The potential for overwhelming loss of personal and family wealth is clear for many people. Although Britain has granted residency rights to fifty thousand families (or approximately 225,000 people) to slow the regrettable migration of talent from Hong Kong, this is not sufficient to meet the needs of the majority of the six million people of Hong Kong. Since most residents have no choice but to accept the outcome, their anxiety is frequently expressed in such defeatist terms as "I don't think about it" or "What can I do?" or "Is this something I have any say about?"

As a side effect to this transition, a question is arising about the political identity of many of the Hong Kong Chinese. British national (overseas) passports are now issued, distinct from the previous British Dependent Territory Citizen passport. With this new classification, some Hong Kong Chinese are identified as British, yet in reality do not have the right to reside in Britain. Over three million of the territory's 5.8 million people fall into this category.

THE ECONOMY

The economy of Hong Kong has grown from an earlier role of financial broker to become a major exporting manufacturer; currently, it is the thirteenth largest trading "country" (city-state) outside of OPEC and COMECON. Several major factors have contributed to and continue to maintain this impressive development, made even more remarkable in the face of its recovery from the worldwide recession of the mid- to late 1970s, the political insecurity generated prior to and during the time of the signing of the Sino-British accord in 1984, and reactions to the crushing of the prodemocracy demonstrations in Beijing's Tienanmen Square.

First, Hong Kong is a free port; therefore, most goods are imported and exported without being taxed. Exceptions are alcohol, tobacco, tobacco products, petroleum products, and soft drinks. Second, the government has not intervened in the control of the banks, financial institutions, and stock and commodities exchange. This degree of noninterference, coined as "positive noninterventionism," has caused many people to consider Hong Kong to be the major financial center of Asia. Third, while any nationality is permitted to build and conduct a business in Hong Kong, no one person or group is permitted to own land since all land is retained by the government (or, in the old British terminology, "The Crown"). Considering the price of land in

Hong Kong, this amounts to extensive wealth. When Hong Kong becomes a Special Administrative Region of China, it will have to share its land-leasing revenues with China. For that reason it behooves both parties to maintain solid property values. Through controlled management of its short- and long-term leases and through the guarantee of all leases and their mortgages to June 30, 2047 (according to the stipulations of the Sino-British Agreement), the government has created the conditions to support stable property values. Fourth, while Hong Kong is considered the classic laissez-faire economy par excellence, its strong centralized government maintains law and order and is strongly committed to subsidized housing. It also owns and manages the airport, the Kowloon-Canton Railroad (KCR), and the Mass Transit Railway (MTR) corporations; has the power to regulate fees for all transportation and utilities; and subsidizes and finances education and a variety of other functions. All in all, the government of Hong Kong is doing an excellent job, while functioning within a budget that consistently produces surpluses.

A crucial economic shift occurred in the late 1980s. As international economic groups consolidated their positions, the United States, previously Hong Kong's major trading partner, relinquished that position to the PRC. While U.S. interests continue to be strong (followed by those of Japan), the PRC has dramatically increased its active participation in Hong Kong, though the precise fiscal and economic dimensions of that participation are unclear. In the late 1980s there were reportedly only five hundred official PRC-related companies registered in Hong Kong, but some analysts put the real number at one thousand and still others surmise that as many as three thousand PRC companies may be invested in Hong Kong. Consequently, since Hong Kong is already currently integrated economically into China, the formal takeover in 1997 may be of less strategic importance—and less traumatic—than had been formerly thought. A clear example of economic integration is the presence of China's holdings on Hong Kong's exchange, demonstrated by the Tian An China listing, the first of the PRC investments to risk the volatility and unpredictability of a capitalistic market.

Integrating the accounting and legal systems of Hong Kong with those of China may prove to be a challenge, but a sense of cooperation has been established in this area as well, as demonstrated by a banking crisis in 1986-87. Four banks were found to be involved in unsound activities, and the PRC's intervention at that time definitely helped to maintain the credibility of Hong Kong's banking system.

Both the current Hong Kong financial analysts and the PRC economists anticipate that Hong Kong's current economic growth will continue at an average rate of 5 percent, thus giving its people one of the highest per capita incomes (approximately $8,000) in the world, which places it fourth in Asia after Brunei, Japan, and Singapore.

EDUCATION

Free schooling is provided for all children up to age fifteen—nine years of education including six years of primary school and three years at the secondary level. This is a major accomplishment considering that 26 percent of Hong Kong's population is of kindergarten or school age. Schools are classified as either Chinese or Anglo-Chinese, depending on whether instruction is in Chinese or English. Some are run by the government; others are subsidized by the government under the guidance of voluntary bodies; still others are private institutions. Frequently, secondary schools are referred to as colleges, so be sure to ask whether a "college" is a secondary school, a junior college, or actually a college of a university. Special services are provided in over seventy schools for the blind, deaf, physically handicapped, emotionally disturbed, and learning disabled.

Education generally follows the traditional Chinese style, relying on rote memorization and repetition as major pedagogical techniques. This style not only limits a student's creative potential but also affects interpersonal relationships. Traditionally, the teacher-student relationship has been one of great respect for the teacher. Teachers are not openly questioned or challenged. Thus, information is accepted uncritically, creativity is not valued, and students are dependent on the teacher as the major source of information. These qualities are later transferred to the work environment, where lower-ranking employees and low-level managers demand clear directives and specific instructions from their supervisors, which they then painstakingly follow. This is a crucial point for Western managers to understand because it is so antithetical to most Western models of education and behavior.

Excellence in education is characteristic of Hong Kong Chinese for several reasons. First, education is easily translated into job opportunity and fiscal stability. Education is perceived as an investment and families will make extensive sacrifices to obtain the best schooling possible. Second, failure in educational endeavors carries with it the loss of face or status, not only for the student but also for the entire family. Finally, those who lack adequate education are seen as somehow "morally deficient." For all these reasons Hong Kong students are subjected to excessive family and societal pressure to achieve. It is not surprising, given the importance of a good education, that competition for placement in the best educational institutions is keen. Admission to private schools in which English is the medium of instruction is increasingly valued.

THE PEOPLE

Of the approximately 5.8 million people in Hong Kong, 97 percent are ethnic Chinese; yet the Chinese are not a homogeneous group. The major group is Cantonese, people who emigrated to Hong Kong or were born of immigrants from Guangdong Province. There are also large communities of Shanghaiese, Hakka, and Tanka, the latter having been forced to leave their traditional life on boats. Within the 3 percent of non-Chinese residents, the Filipino community is the largest (.7 percent), followed by American and British communities (.3 percent each). Other national groups such as Indians, Pakistanis, Japanese, Koreans, Thais, and various Western nationalities make up the final 1 percent. Hong Kong's current population growth rate is 1.2 percent. Population density is approximately 5,000 persons per square kilometer, with some areas exceeding 160,000 persons per square kilometer.

There is and always has been a strong work ethic among the Chinese. Partly because of their cultural heritage and partly because of the needs of a predominantly refugee community, the Hong Kong Cantonese are a strong and hard-working people. Absenteeism is negligible, and there is no tradition of unionism which would polarize industrial disputes and create strikes.

RELIGION

Religion in Hong Kong is steeped in ancient Asian tradition. Buddhism, imported from India in A.D. 1, mingled with indigenous Chinese Taoism, ancient myths and folk beliefs, and Confucianism. The end result was a complicated and frequently confusing religious system.

To ask what Buddhists believe is the wrong question; to ask how one learns to discover the tradition of Buddhism, seek the root of wisdom, and walk the path of personal development is more accurate. Many traditional beliefs have been weakened by the strong influences of urban development and modernization. Religion now takes on more of a ceremonial and ritualized expression—rites during the major festivals, the maintenance of ancestral shrines within the home, and the performance of rites for the dead. Homes and shops have small shrines to protect them from evil, and there are a significant number of Buddhist and Taoist temples used as places to petition the gods. In times of celebration and difficulty, the monks are called upon to offer prayers and exorcisms. Although a large percentage of Hong Kong Chinese have been exposed to Christian values and philosophy through the many religiously affiliated secondary schools, most remain true to traditional Chinese religious thought and practice.

As Hong Kong integrates into the People's Republic of China, religion may become an issue since many of its practices are considered superstitious and are discouraged in the PRC. Of equal interest as 1997 approaches is the role of the Christian community in Hong Kong. The leadership of the major Christian groups—the Hong Kong Christian Council, the Anglican Communion, the Lutheran Church, and the Roman Catholic Church—is Chinese. These indigenous churches serve approximately 10 percent of the population. While the liberalization

policy of the PRC has allowed greater religious tolerance, that tolerance is sure to be tested in 1997.

CLIMATE

Hong Kong is technically subtropical, its climate regulated by
two major monsoons—the winter monsoon from October to April, with
winds from the north or northeast, and the summer monsoon from May
to September, with southerly and southwesterly winds. The most
comfortable season is autumn (October to December), when the
humidity declines and days are generally clear and pleasant. The most
uncomfortable season is the summer monsoon from May to September, when it is hot and sticky with a good deal of rain and occasional
typhoons, especially in August. The average temperature during this
period is ninety degrees Fahrenheit (27° C), with humidity always
somewhere between 80 and 100 percent, making it feel much hotter
than the temperature indicates. Unfortunately, there is no relief at night.
However, hotels, offices, and modern apartments are air-conditioned,
and there are many opportunities to swim and sail. Because of the heat,
it is more comfortable to use umbrellas than raincoats.

Each year Hong Kong weathers a number of typhoons between
the months of May and November. These tropical depressions, with
their extremely high winds and excessive amounts of rainfall, can
create havoc. All storms are well tracked, and Hong Kong has developed an excellent, signal-based warning system communicated by
television and radio broadcasts. A No. 1 signal is a general warning that
a tropical storm is within four hundred miles of Hong Kong; a No. 3
signal indicates severe winds which may exceed sixty knots per hour.
All potted plants and balcony furniture should be brought indoors, and
large objects tied down. Tides may begin to rise, so low-lying areas
should be avoided and provisions to secure boats in a typhoon shelter
or on high ground should be made. When the No. 8 signal is broadcast,
most offices are closed and people immediately return home. All
activities, schools, concerts, and classes are canceled. Due to the risk
of winds gusting up to one hundred knots, all windows should be

covered with typhoon boards and nets or taped to protect them from flying objects. A No. 10 indicates a direct hit on Hong Kong, reminiscent of Typhoon Rose that struck in August 1971, causing extreme damage. As the storm abates, the signals will decrease. It is best to avoid going outside as long as flying objects, flooding, and mud slides are imminent dangers (for more information consult the front pages of your telephone directory). The fun part of a typhoon is the "typhoon party," when friends get together with unexpected time off from work and just enjoy each other's company or, as the Chinese do, play mahjong.

2

Before Leaving

ENTRY REGULATIONS AND DOCUMENTS

A passport, valid for at least six months after entry, is required for all people who wish to enter Hong Kong. Those who possess United Kingdom passports issued in the U.K or those who are citizens of the U.K. or of the colonies by birth, naturalization, registration, or adoption in the U.K., may stay for six months without a visa. Citizens of the British Commonwealth countries, most Western European countries, and a few other nations require visas for a stay exceeding three months. U. S. citizens require a visa for a visit exceeding one month. Citizens of other countries should check with a British consulate for specific regulations that apply to their situation.

All visitors arriving by air must possess a return ticket or arrangements for a continuing flight. Young visitors may be asked to produce evidence that they have sufficient financial support to stay in Hong Kong.

Frequent travelers should secure a multiple-entry visa, which is valid for an extended period of time and allows for repeated visits. Holders of a multiple-entry visa may travel to Macao, the People's Republic of China, or other areas and return to Hong Kong without obtaining another visa. With a single-entry visa, a reentry visa to return to Hong Kong must be obtained for every excursion out of the territory, a time-consuming task best avoided.

Those wanting to live, work, or study in Hong Kong must acquire a referred visa that is processed through the British Consulate in Hong Kong. These are classified as student or employment visas and take six to eight weeks to obtain. Applicants for an employment visa are required to produce an employment contract or a letter of appointment citing salary and benefits. Employment visas are given for different lengths of time, the first usually for a six-month period. Renewals and extensions are somewhat automatic, but the responsibility for initiating the renewal process rests with the applicant. The government will not provide notification of expiration. Failure to apply on time may lead to inconvenience.

The Hong Kong government is highly resistant to changing a person's official status after arrival, so it is imperative that you have your employment and residence visas (and dependent visas for family members) prior to arrival. It is wise to start the process well in advance of departure. Before leaving for Hong Kong, consult with your local British consular office for any recent changes caused by the impending governmental transition.

CUSTOMS REGULATIONS

A word about customs: the key to avoiding customs hassles is to take precautionary measures. If, for example, you bring a great deal of jewelry to Hong Kong, have it listed and an accurate appraisal verified by your local customs office prior to your departure so that when you leave Hong Kong, you will not have any difficulty. All other valuable items such as cameras, watches, and binoculars which have been manufactured outside your country of origin and purchased at home should also be registered with customs to guarantee that you will not have to pay duty on those goods upon repatriation. Sales receipts, appraisals, and repair slips that identify the item as belonging to you before your overseas assignment also constitute valid proof of prior ownership and should be kept in case they are needed. It is also advisable to register furs, though we cannot recommend that you bring them to such a hot, humid climate.

Hong Kong has some specific restrictions. Prohibited items include gold (other than personal jewelry); guns, ammunition, or dangerous weapons; and transceivers such as walkie-talkies or CBs. "Dangerous weapons" include, in addition to the obvious, underwater harpoons, spears, knives, and those wonderful ceremonial swords purchased in other Asian countries.

All medication should be clearly marked. If you are carrying any prescription drug which is a narcotic or may have a "street value," obtain a supporting letter from your physician or a copy of the prescription. Hong Kong has strict laws related to the use of nonprescription drugs and narcotics, and any possession is reason for arrest and prosecution. While the consequences are not as serious as the required death penalty of some Southeast Asian countries, they are severe.

Customs clearance of your personal goods sent by air or sea freight to Hong Kong is relatively uncomplicated. Your moving agents can best advise you of any specific requirements that are unique to your situation. Should you wish to import a car, there will be a "first registration tax" placed on it based on the value of the car (for further information on importing and buying vehicles, see chapter 10). There are no restrictions on goods taken out of Hong Kong, but you must have a bill of sale for major art objects or antiques. Detailed information on customs regulations can be obtained from the Hong Kong Tourist Board.

HEALTH REGULATIONS

Officials are strict about health regulations. Booster shots for all the inoculations that are common in the United States and Europe are recommended as well as diphtheria and tetanus. Cholera shots are required only if you have passed through an infected area during the fourteen days prior to your arrival. Before you leave Hong Kong to travel elsewhere in Asia, seek the advice of your local Hong Kong doctor concerning specific health requirements for other Asian countries.

IMPORTING PETS

Both dogs and cats are subject to a thirty-day quarantine at your expense in either a government-sponsored or a private kennel. For all animals, including birds, gerbils, and hamsters, you must obtain a landing permit and provide your Hong Kong airline with special information about your pet at least one week before arrival. You will also need a quarantine or import permit from the senior veterinary officer of the Agriculture and Fisheries Department. If you are seriously considering taking your pets, contact the Hong Kong officials at the nearest consulate well in advance of your departure.

Some people have strong feelings about importing pets. While the keepers at the quarantine kennels are kind to the animals and you can visit them daily if you wish, it is still no kindness to your pet to subject it to long airline flights in cargo and the isolating kennel experience. If you want a pet, wait until you arrive in Hong Kong. There are many places to purchase a wide variety—pet shops, the Kennel Club, and private breeders who advertise in the *South China Morning Post.* The Royal Society for Prevention of Cruelty to Animals frequently has pets that are more than happy to share their lives with a newly arrived family. With proper papers and shots, your Hong Kong pet can easily follow you home when your tour in Hong Kong is over.

CLOTHING

In general, the Hong Kong Chinese are more formal than many westerners regarding their dress, and they set the tone for westerners in Hong Kong. Plan for summer clothes most of the year along with a lightweight coat or sweater. Short sleeves are acceptable during the hot months, but skimpy tank tops and shorts should be reserved for the beach or sports activities. Most people like sandals not only because they are cool but also because they allow the feet to sweat in the heat. Even during the hottest months, women may need wraps or jackets for air-conditioned buildings.

The winter season is variable. Two days of glove-wearing weather can be followed by sunny, balmy days in the high 70s (21° C) and low 80s (24° C). A wool dress or two for women and lightweight wool suits for professional men and women are needed for the cooler days, and winter evenings can get cold enough to warrant warm jackets, gloves, and scarves. The best advice is to be prepared for temperature changes during winter and early spring. Wear layers of clothes during the early colder hours of the day which can be removed as the day warms up and put back on during the chillier late afternoon and early evening. Most houses and apartments are unheated during the cold season, and people rely on small electric or gas space heaters. There are times when warm night clothes are desirable.

Professional and social dress is quite formal. Men wear dark suits all year for business. Coats and ties for men and nice dresses for women are usually worn for dinner in restaurants and frequently at dinner parties, and there are occasions when formal attire is worn. Rather conservative sportswear is needed in quantity for frequent changes during muggy weather.

Most items of clothing are available ready-made in Hong Kong, but larger Western sizes for men and women may be difficult to find, particularly in shoes (above size 7 for women) and undergarments. Many expatriate women purchase their clothes at specialized shops in Hong Kong that carry Western sizes or at home during home leave. Hong Kong tailors are world-renowned for their ability to copy garments. Women merely need to give a picture to their tailor to have a copy made. Maternity clothes are not readily available.

FURNISHINGS

Westerners living in Hong Kong strongly advise incoming expatriates to leave most of their furniture at home and buy locally made rattan, wrought iron, teak, and rosewood furniture that holds up well in the humid climate. If the local style does not appeal to you, there is also a wide variety of stores in the major shopping centers in Hong Kong and Kowloon that specialize in imported American, European, and Asian furniture, so the selection is quite complete. Don't bring furniture or decorative items to Hong Kong that you would regret having damaged by the humidity. The moisture is very hard on rugs, books, files, and upholstered furniture, which can suffer from mold and insects. Air conditioners help, as do dehumidifiers and dehumidifying crystals placed in bureau drawers and closets. But it is very damp. Many people install bar heaters (of low electrical wattage) in at least one closet to protect cameras, film, special clothes, leather goods, and so on, from mold.

You will, of course, want to take a few small pieces of furniture and some decorative items that will survive the climate and add a touch of home, such as small tables, extra lamps, and mirrors. Draperies from home seldom fit the much larger Hong Kong windows, and drapery fabrics can be purchased easily in decorator shops or the shopping lanes.

Most expatriate housing is roomy and open. When moving into an unfurnished flat, even those which are considered luxurious, you will have to supply everything—air conditioners, refrigerators, stoves, curtain rods, even light fixtures. Occasionally, you will rent a flat previously occupied by an expatriate, from whom you may be able to buy many of these items. People in Hong Kong entertain formally, so be sure to bring the china and crystal pieces that complement your style. However, should you not wish to chance damaging the family heirlooms, you can find many traditional and contemporary Asian patterns locally. Most expatriates choose to hire household help. While those who fill such jobs are generally careful, they may not have the same sense of caution for your favorite china as you have. Beds and linens are two more items you may want to bring with you since Chinese, British, and American sizes are all different. You can, of course, find beds and mattresses in Hong Kong, but most expatriates choose not to return home with them since it will be difficult to find sheets that fit.

Another good way of quickly furnishing your home is to follow the advertisements in the supermarkets, the local newspaper, the *Dollar Saver,* and *The Kowloon Advertiser* for secondhand furniture and appliances since the expatriate population is constantly on the move. The book *Living in Hong Kong* (published by the American Chamber of

Commerce in Hong Kong) and the Community Advice Bureau, a group that provides a hot line service, have lists of shops that are helpful to the newly arrived expatriate.

ELECTRICITY AND APPLIANCES

Electric current in Hong Kong is 200 volts, 50 cycles, phases 1,3 and is quite stable. If your appliances are wired for 110 volts, they can be used with a transformer. Small transformers are easy to buy, and large ones can be made to order. No synchronous 60-cycle appliances such as clocks, record players, or tape recorders will work on 50 cycles. Some expatriates choose to have their 60-cycle appliances changed to 50 prior to leaving home. If you plan to remain in Hong Kong for a long assignment, you may wish to purchase all your appliances there. A wide range of European, Japanese, and Hong Kong appliances is available. If you plan to rent, keep in mind that kitchen appliances (refrigerators, washers and driers, stoves) are not supplied in a furnished apartment. Electric stoves are discouraged; most people use local gas stoves that are suited to Hong Kong gas. Purchasing used appliances is a popular alternative to buying new ones. Look for classified ads in the local paper as well as bulletin boards, supermarkets, clubs, and the *Dollar Saver* and *The Kowloon Advertiser.* Your hot water is usually supplied by a gas-fueled *geyser,* a British term for a water heater. Geysers heat water on an as-needed basis and are not designed to store hot water. If your geyser is located in your bathroom, as most are, be sure to open your bathroom window or door to provide ventilation for the noxious gas that is generated. With appropriate ventilation this system is quite effective and safe. Electric water heaters have recently become popular.

European-style washing machines that have their own capacity to heat water are the preferred model in Hong Kong. American models that require furnace-heated water are not functional.

3

On Arrival

Relocating to Hong Kong is a stressful, draining experience. Soon after your arrival, you must both establish yourself professionally and find a home, be it a temporary or permanent one. *Living in Hong Kong,* mentioned above, is a valuable resource in this process, and is available at most English-language bookstores in Hong Kong. Developed by long-term expatriates in Hong Kong, it contains information that will help you adjust to the social and business life of the territory and includes current addresses and telephone numbers which will be especially useful during your stay. It also includes a section on living in Beijing.

AIRPORT INFORMATION

Prior to landing, a conventional immigration form will be given to you and then collected by the immigration officer upon arrival. Ground transportation to all locations is easily obtainable because of the airport's central location. Directly outside of customs in Buffer Hall, arrange for liveried pickup service at a hotel information desk or ask for the Airport Hire Car service with its chauffeur-driven, fixed-rate cars. Two other options are also available. One is the Airbus, which services three routes, all with pickups every fifteen minutes: Route A1, servicing Tsim Sha Tsui in Kowloon; Route A2, servicing the Central District hotels; and Route A3, servicing Causeway Bay. The rate is posted on the bus sign when you board. This service stops at most of the major hotels in the assigned areas. You will need exact change, which you can get at the service kiosk in the terminal before boarding.

The last option is a metered taxi (look for the rate card inside the cab and at the sign posted at the taxi stand). You will be charged a set initial fee and an additional rate for every 0.25 km after the first two kilometers, plus a one-dollar charge for each piece of luggage. You will also want to tip the driver approximately 10 percent of the fare. The average fare to hotels in the Central or Causeway Bay districts runs approximately HK$45-$55, which includes the HK$20 surcharge for all trips by taxi through the cross-harbor tunnel. Most drivers have some knowledge of English and are acquainted with major hotels and office buildings. They also generally know addresses of residences, but it is advisable to carry the street address written in Chinese characters in case the driver needs it.

IDENTIFICATION CARD

A law introduced in 1980 to curb illegal immigration requires all Hong Kong residents, including expatriates, to carry an identity document at all times. Everyone over the age of eleven with resident status must register with the director of immigration to receive a Hong Kong identification card. Juvenile identity cards are issued to those between the ages of eleven and eighteen. Nonresident visitors are required to carry a passport or some other form of identification. You must apply in person for the ID card within thirty days after arrival in Hong Kong or at the age of eighteen at one of the ten registration offices in Hong Kong. Bring a passport (and a photocopy of the first five pages) or birth certificate, two recent photos, and school records of your children. Parents may apply for their children, but the children must personally appear at the registration office. The card will not be issued unless one of the parents has an employment visa. For exact locations of the registration centers as well as additional information, you may write, call, or visit the Immigration Department, Wanchai Tower II, 7 Gloucester Road, Wanchai, Hong Kong; tel: 8256111; cable: MIGRATION HONGKONG; telex: 45656. You will also want to register with your home consulate.

HOTELS

It is always a good idea to arrange your hotel accommodations prior to your arrival in Hong Kong, but it is especially important if you plan to arrive during the peak tourist season (October-January). There is a wide range of hotels appealing to a spectrum of tastes and budgets. If you are relocating your family, a hotel stay can be a pleasant little holiday or an ordeal of uncertainty since there is frequently a delay of several weeks before household goods and furniture arrive. Choose your hotel carefully and consider the availability of transportation to office and school, recreational facilities (pool, tennis, etc.), room size, air-conditioning, and accessibility to entertainment. Leave flats, discussed later in chapter 7, are also a viable alternative for interim housing.

For information on hotels, contact the nearest office of the Hong Kong Trade Development Council or the Hong Kong Tourist Association, which are located in Amsterdam, Barcelona, Frankfurt, Hamburg, London, Milan, Paris, Stockholm, Vienna, and Zurich in Europe; Chicago, Dallas, Los Angeles, New York, and Toronto in North America; Panama in Central America; Beijing, Osaka, Shanghai, Singapore, and Tokyo in Asia; Sydney in Australia; and Dubai in the Middle East. Consult your local Yellow Pages for the area offices or contact the head office at Hong Kong Trade Development Council, Great Eagle Center, 31st Floor, 23 Harbour Road, Hong Kong; tel: 8334333; cable: CONOTRAD HONGKONG; telex: 73595 CONHK HX; fax: 852-730249.

SETTLING-IN SERVICES

One major company and many property management groups provide settling-in services. Hong Kong Orientations (tel: 8129281) provides a professional relocation counselor whose sole responsibility is to help the transferees to become familiarized with Hong Kong, its shopping and its community resources. This service helps to minimize the transition stress. Many expatriates use such services when visiting Hong Kong on a predeparture familiarization trip, and then contract them for an additional ten to twenty hours of personalized service upon arrival.

TRANSPORTATION

Car Rentals

Hong Kong is very congested, so most short-term visitors rely on taxis or public transportation. Many long-term expatriates maintain or hire chauffeur-driven cars; fewer drive rental cars, although Japanese models are available for the daring. To rent a car, you need to be twenty-five years of age and have a valid national driver's license. In lieu of a national license, an international driver's licence obtained through your local Automobile Association before your departure will do. All the major hotels as well as international agencies, such as Avis and National, offer rental services. There is usually a three-hour minimum with an additional hourly rate. Local companies are considerably cheaper.

Be sure to acquaint yourself with the highway code of Hong Kong prior to driving. The Government Information Service publishes a small booklet that you should read. Also, keep in mind that all traffic moves on the left-hand side of the street, which takes some getting used to for the uninitiated (see chapter 10 for more information on cars and driving).

Taxis

Metered taxis are cheap and accessible and the quickest way to travel through the crowded streets of Hong Kong. Taxis can be easily spotted by their colors—red with silver roofs—and are often air-conditioned. Taxis in the New Territories are green and white, and taxis on Lantau are blue and have a different rate system. Check the card posted inside the vehicle. Drivers usually know enough English to get you to well-known locations, but if you are going anywhere out of the ordinary, it is advisable, as mentioned before, to have the address and directions written in Chinese. See above regarding fares and tipping. An additional surcharge is required when you travel through the Cross Harbor Tunnel and the Aberdeen and Lion Rock Tunnels, or if you have luggage or extra large parcels. To catch a taxi, you can wait your turn at one of the many taxi stands throughout the territory, call a radio-controlled taxi (there is an additional charge for these), or hail one in the street. Drivers are not permitted, however, to pick up passengers in areas that are marked by yellow curbs. Consult the Yellow Pages for taxi services. There is no need to tip taxi drivers, but passengers round out the fare to the nearest dollar.

You may notice taxis waiting at the side of the road or driving around with a cloth over the meter. These taxis are off-duty. In actuality, however, during rush hour, late at night, or at peak holiday seasons, it is often a signal that the driver may wish to bargain a fare. This is illegal, but it is a fairly common occurrence. Other taxis will place a card saying "Hong Kong" or "Kowloon" over their meter, indicating that they wish to secure a fare which would return them to their side of Hong Kong. If you use their services, you will pay less for using the Cross Harbor Tunnel.

In addition to the regular taxis, there are *pak pais,* somewhat illegal taxis with "white plates," which are usually found in residential areas. These carriers operate as contracted drivers, in comparison to the metered official taxis, so it is important to negotiate your fee prior to entering the vehicle.

If you feel that you have been treated unfairly at the hands of a taxi driver, note the taxi number and call the twenty-four-hour special hot line (5277177) to gain assistance from the Royal Hong Kong Police.

MTR

The MTR connects Hong Kong Island and Kowloon. The 38.6-kilometer (twenty-four-mile) system has three lines—Kwun Tong, Tsuen Wan, and Island—operates thirty-seven stations between Sheung Wan Station and Chai Wan on Hong Kong Island and between Kwun Tong and Tsuen Wan in Kowloon, and runs from 6:00 A.M. to 1:00 A.M. By securing an MTR map, you can pinpoint the major business and recreational centers since most are located near MTR stations. The *MTR Guide Book* and the *MTR Leisure Guide* available at all MTR stations are valuable resources for mastering the system. Ticket prices are based on distance and destination rather than a flat fare, and all ticket machines are well marked as to the price of the ticket you must purchase to reach your specific destination. The ticket machines will take only exact change, and although there are a few change machines located in the stations, you will save considerable time and energy by having change with you.

Your ticket, a magnetic plastic card, is used to enter the turnstiles to board the system. It is immediately returned to you to be kept in your possession during the ride and deposited in the turnstile when exiting. If you purchase a stored-value ticket costing HK$50 to HK$200 at the station banks, your ticket will be returned to you as you leave the exit turnstile. The exit machine will indicate how much money remains on your card. The system is clean and efficient and a reliable means of rapid transportation. There are no toilets available within the system, and smoking, drinking, and eating are prohibited. Also, you may not board the system with large pieces of luggage.

Buses, Minibuses, and Maxicabs

Two bus companies operate in Hong Kong: China Motor Bus Company (blue in color) on Hong Kong Island and the Kowloon Motor

Bus Company (red in color) in Kowloon and the New Territories. Buses are an inexpensive means of transportation, and they travel anywhere in the territory, although at a rather slow pace. Both systems operate from six in the morning until midnight each day. Drivers do not give change, so exact change is required. The buses operate on a flat-fee basis, regardless of distance, and customers deposit their fees upon boarding. There are some air-conditioned, deluxe buses and express buses that guarantee a seat. Commuters from the Repulse Bay and Stanley areas have found that the bus service is practical and efficient; it saves the commuter from the frustrations of driving, is less expensive than private taxis, and is comfortable (providing you have a seat). Since most bus stops accommodate a number of different routes, the drivers will not know which people wish to board their buses. Be sure to flag the bus by raising your hand; otherwise, the driver may pass without stopping, thinking you are waiting for a different bus. All buses post their destinations in English and Chinese. All route numbers followed by the letter *M* indicate that the bus will take you to an MTR station, the letter *K* to a railroad station. An *R* means that the bus only operates on holidays.

Van-sized minibuses and maxicabs, also called public light buses, provide an alternative to private cars, taxis, and buses. Their fare is slightly higher than the larger buses, yet considerably cheaper than a taxi. Minibuses (yellow, sixteen-seater vans with a red stripe) travel along main routes and make unscheduled stops. Their fares are posted on a sign hung in the front window. A sign on the roof indicates their final destination. Fares are paid upon entering and are based on the distance and the number of seats available to pick up new passengers. Your price is the price that is posted at the time of boarding the vehicle. These vehicles cannot pick up or discharge passengers at bus stops or at certain other restricted areas. Maxicabs (sixteen-seater vans distinguished by a green stripe on the side and a green roof) have fixed routes and fixed schedules. Many of these minibuses and maxicabs operate in the Mid-Levels just above Central and in areas not easily reached by public transportation. When you wish to board, raise your hand to flag the driver.

Trams

Built in 1904, the tram system, with its picturesque trams, runs from 5:40 A.M. to 1:00 A.M. along the Hong Kong Island's northern shoreline, or at least what was once the shoreline prior to the extensive reclamation work. The thirty-four-kilometer trip passes through some of the most interesting areas of Hong Kong, offering wonderful views to the rider who sits by the front, second-level window. The sounds, smells, and excitement of Hong Kong are at your fingertips. The trams are best utilized for leisurely pleasure trips—they are extremely slow. Even walking may be quicker.

If you live in certain sections of the Mid-Levels or at Victoria Peak, the Peak Tram (actually a funicular railway first built in 1888) provides a fast and inexpensive means of transportation up and down the mountainside. It also offers some of the most scenic views of Hong Kong Harbor. The tram stops at four points prior to reaching the Peak Tower, which houses a restaurant, shops, and an observation station. Service runs from seven in the morning to midnight. A trip on the Peak Tram at night is a must for your visiting friends and relatives.

Ferries

Ferries have been and continue to be a reliable source of transportation in Hong Kong, functional not only for harbor crossings but also providing access to areas not reachable by other means of transportation, such as Discovery Bay, a large, modern, residential community on Lantau. Another advantage of using the ferry service is that it offers a restful reprieve from the traffic congestion, allowing one to appreciate the breeze, fresh air, and the incredibly beautiful scenery of the sea and shore that are the hallmarks of Hong Kong. There are two ferry companies, the Star Ferry and the Hong Kong and Yaumati Ferry Company.

The Star Ferry, established in 1898, is best known since it connects Queens Pier in Central (the heart of Hong Kong Island) and Wanchai with Ocean Terminal at Tsim Sha Tsui in Kowloon. The trip, costing a very modest sum, passes through the center of the harbor and features a lively, water-level view of the busy harbor. It is picturesque and enjoyable, experienced either from the crowded lower deck or the more spacious first-class deck.

The Hong Kong and Yaumati Ferry Company operates the major ferry services connecting Hong Kong Island with other sections of the Kowloon Peninsula and the major outlying islands. Its ships range from small water buses to double- and triple-decker ships. Hovercraft are used for the more distant routes. Obtain schedules for the various services. Ferries leaving for the outlying islands depart from the piers west of the Star Ferry Pier, near Jubilee Street. The islands are enjoyable places for one-day outings, for hiking, and for picnics.

The considerable Hong Kong/Macao and Hong Kong/Guangzhou traffic is transported by jetfoil, hydrofoil, and steamer ferries. schedules may be secured from the Hong Kong/Macao and Far East Hydrofoil offices in Hong Kong.Walla Wallas are motorized sampans named after Walla Walla, Washington, where the engines were made originally. They can be hired at the Central and Tsim Sha Tsui terminals to accommodate late-hour harbor crossings after conventional transportation has closed for the night.

Kowloon-Canton Railroad

The major function of this 32.3-kilometer (twenty-mile) railroad is to connect Hong Kong and the Kwai Chung Container Port with the major rail system of the PRC. The train is also a good transportation option for people living in Shatin as well as a way of traveling to Chinese University in the New Territories. Local service of the KCR runs from Hung Hom Railroad Station in Kowloon to the Chinese border, terminating at Sheung Shui, the last station in the territory. Trains entering China continue through the border at Lo Wu, with its famous bridge to Guangzhou Province. Be sure to disembark at the Sheung Shui Station unless you have a visa to travel to Guangzhou or to the industrial center in Shenzhen. (There are no toilet facilities on the KCR trains.)

The Hong Kong government, through its Government Publications Centre, offers *The Guide to Hong Kong's Bus, Light Bus, Rail and Ferry Service,* a comprehensive annual listing of the routes, fares, and schedules of all the above-mentioned means of transportation.

FINANCIAL MATTERS

Currency

The Hong Kong dollar is the national currency. Notes issued by the Hong Kong and Shanghai Banking Corporation and the Standard Chartered Bank come in the following denominations: HK$10 (green), $20 (orange), $50 (blue), $100 (red), $500 (brown) and $ 1,000 (gold). Do not be concerned if some of the bills of the same denomination are not the same size since smaller notes are being introduced. The lowest denomination is the one-cent note, which makes a perfect memento of Hong Kong to share with friends and family from home but is worthless otherwise. The government mints coins in denominations of 10c, 20c, 50c, $1, $2, and $5. The Hong Kong dollar should not be equated with the U.S. or Canadian dollar. At the current rate, US$1 equals approximately HK$7.80. Tales are frequently told of taxi rides that cost US$50 when in actuality they cost only HK$50 (or US$6.40).

Banking and Exchange

A major international financial center, Hong Kong has over 150 licensed banks with more than 1,400 branch offices. While hours are not uniformly set, banks are generally open from 9:00 A.M. to 4:30 P.M. on weekdays and 9:00 A.M. to 12:30 P.M. on Saturdays. A full range of banking services is provided in Hong Kong dollars, including savings accounts, checking accounts, deposits, loans, and remittances. Some banks offer Autopay, an automatic service designed to facilitate payment of utilities and other personal bills. It may be difficult to obtain a checking account in your national currency, but you can open a savings account in that currency and purchase drafts for overseas mailing.

Hong Kong has no central bank. Instead, a commissioner of banking exercises general supervision over banking practices. Funds can move in and out of Hong Kong without restrictions of any kind. In 1972 all exchange controls were abolished, permitting total flexibility in the movement of capital and the repatriation of profits.

Credit Cards, Traveler's Checks, and Personal Checks

Most places accept credit cards: VISA, Diners Club, Master-Card, JCB, Carte Blanche, and American Express. When using cash, ask for the "cash discount." After negotiating a price, you may find some resistance from the merchant to accepting a credit card after the "bottom cash price" has been agreed upon. The merchant may try to add an additional 7 percent on the price of the item once you produce your card. This practice is illegal, and if the merchant continues to insist, you have the option of reporting the incident to the police.

Traveler's checks, issued in dollars, pounds, or yen, are widely accepted. As elsewhere in the world, exchange rates will fluctuate depending on your choice of a bank, money changer, hotel, or major retail outlet. When exchanging currency or traveler's checks, expect to have a small charge added. However, many merchants value traveler's checks, so try to negotiate with the merchant for a more positive exchange rate or favorable purchase price.

Personal checks drawn on your home bank will be of little use. Some retailers may accommodate their customers, but it is not the accepted practice. It is advisable to open a Hong Kong-dollar checking account; local Hong Kong checks are accepted readily. The check-writing system of Hong Kong is similar to that of Great Britain. If a check is not "crossed," it is considered a "bearer" check, which allows anyone to cash it without endorsing it. You can order checks with the word "bearer" deleted; otherwise, to protect yourself, cross a check by making two parallel lines in the upper left-hand corner and blacken out "bearer." Ask someone to show you how this is done. Never, however, cross a check if you are cashing it for yourself. As is true elsewhere, all alterations on a check must be initialed. One more piece of advice: when writing out the amount of the check, be sure to end the amount with the word *only* (seven hundred dollars and twenty-five cents only).

Bank Cards

Several of the major banks provide bank cards for the withdrawal of funds. Generally, a cardholder may withdraw up to two thousand dollars per day from current accounts and one thousand dollars per day from savings accounts. Selected banks also allow their clients to make transfers and deposits with the cards. The EPS or Easy Pay System is another convenience available through most banks to facilitate the immediate transfer of funds from your accounts to those of your creditors; it makes many commercial and entertainment transactions extremely easy.

Tipping

Hotels and many modern restaurants add a 10 percent surcharge to your bill for service. If you feel the service was particularly special, add an additional 5 percent. Tips are expected in traditional Chinese restaurants, where a service charge may not be included. Be sure to inquire before paying your bill. It is customary to leave an additional amount of small change in settling the bill. Small tips of HK$5 to HK$10 are appropriate for service in hotels for porters and barbers.

COMMUNICATION

Newspapers and Periodicals

There are four English-language newspapers in Hong Kong: the *South China Morning Post,* the *Hong Kong Standard, The Asian Wall Street Journal,* and the *International Herald Tribune.* Each paper has its own style and orientation. The Asian editions of *Time, Newsweek,* and *Reader's Digest* are produced in Hong Kong, as are the *Far Eastern Economic Review, Asian Business, Asiaweek,* and other publications focusing on the Pacific rim. Other English publications include *Asiamoney, Asian Finance, Asian Medical News, Business Traveller, Far East Business, Hong Kong, Inc., Hong Kong Trader, Sunday Examiner, Textile Asia, Travel Directory,* and *The Asian Man-*

ager. All the major American, Australian, English, and European magazines can be found at newsstands and bookstores throughout Hong
Kong, although delays of a month or two are common. Magazines of
special interest to newcomers are *Arts of Asia, Orientations, Connois-
seur's Asia,* and the *Hong Kong Tattler.*

Telephone

Telephone service is automatic and efficient. Domestic equipment can be ordered from the Hong Kong Telephone Company Limited. Order your phone as soon as you know your permanent address to
avoid any delay in installation. It is wise to be present when the phone
system is installed so that phones are placed according to your wishes.
The telephone company publishes an English commercial and consumer directory as well as three residential directories, one for each
area (Hong Kong, Kowloon, and the New Territories). These directories
will help you not only in finding needed telephone numbers but also in
locating the many other resources required in establishing yourself in
Hong Kong.

All telephone listings include seven digits. Do not use the area
codes that were in effect in the territory prior to 1990: Hong Kong-5,
Kowloon-3, and New Territory-0.

Most shops and restaurants allow customers to use their phones.
There is no charge, and a polite thank you to the proprietor is sufficient
when you are finished. Public pay telephones (bright red) are numerous and inexpensive.

International Direct Dialing (IDD) is available, but you must
apply for the service. A special code book will be supplied, and all
charges are then billed to your home number.

Call 999 for emergencies requiring help from the police department, the fire department, or an ambulance.

Television

Hong Kong has two commercial stations: Television Broadcast
Ltd. (popularly known as TVB) and Asia Television Ltd., or ATV. Both
stations provide English- and Chinese-language programs ranging

from Chinese and Western soap operas to epic historical productions to local variety and talent shows and movies. The English productions created in Hong Kong are augmented by programs from the United States, Great Britain, and many of the Commonwealth countries. Unfortunately, there is a time lag of several months to a year before foreign programs are shown in Hong Kong.

The government-owned Radio Television Hong Kong (RTHK) produces educational and public affairs programs focusing on civic education, adult education, and programs for children and youth. When one considers that over 90 percent of all households in Hong Kong own at least one television set, the impact of television is significant.

The Educational Television Service (ETV) provides telecasts to primary and secondary schools for educational purposes. Programs are intended to complement classroom teaching in the four basic subject areas of Chinese, English, mathematics, and social studies in primary and secondary schools, with the addition of science at the secondary or high school level.

A word of caution to Americans. Remember that American-made television sets will not receive Hong Kong transmission signals since they use a rediffusion system. But if you expect to use either professional or homemade American videotapes while you are in Hong Kong, bring your American-made television and VCR specifically for this reason and plan to buy a local set as well.

Radio Broadcasting

Radio Television Hong Kong and commercial radio provide the basic audio broadcasting. The British Forces Broadcasting Service also provides an alternative.

RTHK is subsidized by the government and broadcasts Chinese programs on three of its five channels. Radio 3 provides English programming, and radio 4 broadcasts bilingual programs of fine music. BBC World Service is available on Radio 5 during specific hours. Mandarin programs and services for other minority groups may be heard on RTHK. Around-the-clock news services are available as well as emergency services, which are helpful during typhoon season.

Commercial radio's three channels provide a variety of programs, all supported by advertising. These channels also broadcast a wide range of outdoor events such as pop concerts and the Community Chest walks.

A radio will provide you with companionship as you travel or, more likely, when you are stuck in your car in traffic. Hong Kong talk shows also provide a vehicle for expressing personal opinions. Many talk shows use telephone calls as an integral part of their broadcast, thus giving the courageous expatriate a forum to express a viewpoint. It's fun and one quickly understands the issues and outlooks of expatriates in Hong Kong by listening to the concerns of the community. Another value of radio is the Cantonese study service, which will help you in your study of Chinese.

Postal Services

Mail service in Hong Kong is quite adequate, with a guaranteed delivery of late afternoon postings the following day. Overseas airmail will take three to five days. "Speedpost" is a special mailing service for rapid delivery overseas. Your local post office can give you a leaflet listing its services and current rates. The main post office in Hong Kong is next to the Star Ferry. In Kowloon, it is on Peking Road, opposite the Ocean Center. These offices provide all mailing services as well as the buying and cashing of postal orders. In addition there are well over one hundred local post offices throughout Hong Kong.

If you plan to send any parcels, acquaint yourself with current regulations since there are certain weight requirements. Sea mail is by far the most economical parcel service, but it is slow, requiring from seven to ten weeks for delivery to North America. Prior to the holiday season, check the postal service notices for final posting dates required to guarantee the parcel's arrival in North and South America, Europe, and Africa. Any goods sent out of Hong Kong must have a customs declaration.

DATES AND MEASURES

The Hong Kong system of writing dates is day, month, year, not the month-day-year sequence common to the United States. Therefore 3/2/91 is read as the third of February, and not as the second day of March.

Measurements can be confusing. In the 1980s Hong Kong began the transition from the old British system to the metric system. Adding to the complexity, many people use the Chinese system of measurement. For example, one *tsi* equals approximately four grams, one *leung* or *tael* equals 1.3 ounces, one *gah* or *catty* equals 1.3 pounds, and 2.4 *chek* equals one yard. These numbers will be used in Hong Kong food markets, so be aware that when you ask for a pound of something, you will more than likely get a catty, which will give you one-third more produce than you may have wanted. Most other shops will use the International System of Units, or S.I., which is the official metric system. Until you catch on, it is best to carry a small conversion card.

4

Language

Although Hong Kong has two official languages, realistically speaking the major language is Chinese. At the time of its colonization, English became the only official language. It was not until the mid-1940s that Chinese was recognized as an official language.

There are a number of Chinese dialects, many of which are barely intelligible to speakers of another dialect. Because of its proximity to Guangzhou, Cantonese is the dominant spoken dialect of the majority of people in Hong Kong, followed by Mandarin. In addition to these two major dialects there are multiple regional subdialects. This diversity of spoken language comes from the territorial isolation of the provinces of China during the early centuries of its development. Linguistic diversity has contributed significantly to the frustration of efforts to bring national unity to China and has fostered intense regional and provincial rivalries. Like most immigrant people, the Chinese tended to seek out their own linguistic and cultural groups when they came to Hong Kong, such as the Hakka people in the farming areas of the New Territories and the Haklo boat people in Aberdeen. In other areas, like Rennie Mills, Mandarin dominates since the original settlers of that area were members of the Nationalist forces who fled from China at the time of the revolution. It is not uncommon for a Chinese colleague to use English in his work, Cantonese in negotiating everyday life and relating to his children's school, a regional dialect with family and in-laws, and Mandarin to signify his level of education as well as his interest in the life and business of the People's Republic of China.

The major unifying feature of Chinese on the mainland, and to a lesser degree in Hong Kong, is the written word since written Chinese is the same regardless of the spoken dialect. Basically following the Mandarin language structure, written Chinese provides a common medium of communication for all literate people.

LEARNING CHINESE

Mandarin, the official dialect of the People's Republic and of the Republic of China and the major dialect of Singapore, is not widely spoken in Hong Kong. Mandarin, or *Putunghua* (ordinary language), developed in the region of Beijing. All educated Chinese study Mandarin, but the level of fluency may vary. Because Mandarin is the official dialect of the PRC, its use will understandably increase after 1997; Mandarin is currently being taught in Hong Kong schools.

Any Chinese dialect is difficult to learn. Fortunately, expatriates can usually communicate in English since it is normally spoken by the Chinese associated with business and the tourist industry in Hong Kong. Nonetheless, a working knowledge of spoken Chinese or even just a few commonly used greetings will enhance both your business and social relationships. Since Guangdong Province has three of China's special economic zones, the status of Cantonese is increasing in importance within China. Although knowledge of Putunghua is still important, knowledge of Cantonese is becoming increasingly valuable.

For the short-term visitor, a realistic language goal is to memorize several of the conversational or survival phrases in Cantonese: greetings, such as *Ni hou ma?* (How are you?) or *Jou san* (Good morning); the polite language of hospitality and of giving and receiving gifts; the numbering system; and phrases for asking the price of goods, using a taxi, finding a rest room, and so on.

Unfortunately, Chinese not only has a multiplicity of dialects; it is also a tonal language. If you do not have a good ear for differentiating tones and an ability to repeat them accurately, you will have a frustrating time learning Cantonese and Mandarin. Cantonese, the more difficult, contains seven major tones (nine according to some experts): high, middle, low, high rising, high falling, low rising, and low falling. Mandarin has five major tones: high, low, high falling, middle rising, and low rising. It is a challenge to try to utter some of the unique sounds of Cantonese, such as the low rising tone of *ng.* In the end, the process of learning Chinese is basically a matter of memorization and practice. Learning tones and gaining confidence for even elementary use of the language can take well over a year of hard work, but if you undertake to do it, that work will pay off. First of all, your respect among your Hong Kong colleagues will be significantly enhanced, and second, you will be able to avoid using the wrong tone for a word like *ma* and end up calling someone's mother a horse.

Learning spoken Chinese normally involves using a romanized text. Unfortunately, there are many romanizations used in Hong Kong, some following the British phonetic system, others the American. This diversification of romanized texts can be frustrating. Our advice is to begin with one system and stay with it.

Although most bookstores have basic Cantonese and Mandarin language texts and tapes for self-study, the best approach, if you are at all serious about learning Chinese, is to enroll in a course at the university or attend the Mandarin or Cantonese courses offered by the YMCA or YWCA. A basic course will lay the foundation of tones. After mastering the tonal system, arrange to have a tutor or some Chinese friend help you with conversation. Without a systemized approach to the tonal system, you will be severely handicapped in your efforts.

Learning to read and write in Chinese is time-consuming. To be even minimally competent, you will need to learn at least 1,200 basic characters. Not only would you have to memorize the characters for recognition, you would also have to painstakingly learn to write the characters, many of which require up to twenty brush strokes, all placed in a precise order and sequence. Chinese is a monosyllabic language. Each syllable is an idea and each idea is expressed by a character. Some characters are picture graphs. The word for "woman," for example, looks like a woman bending a little, which is the cultural view of woman's social position. The character for "good" is that of a woman and a male child. Thus, some characters combine a series of characters to portray an idea. Have people point out to you the basic survival characters, such as exits and male and female washrooms. While most places have signs in English and Chinese, some areas have only Chinese, and knowing these basic characters is helpful. It is also wise to learn the character(s) for your country and to include them on the letters and packages you send home. This will speed your mail through the postal system.

USING ENGLISH

A common mistake that we often make when speaking with persons who are not native speakers of our language is to talk too fast and too loudly; to make reference to current national events, sports, and entertainment; and to use idioms, analogies, and proverbs, all of which demand a knowledge of the culture the person does not have. Some people believe that if they shout, their meaning will be better understood. Just speak clearly and a little bit more slowly than usual. Above all, be patient and don't hesitate either to repeat a word or phrase or to ask a local person to do the same. Always allow more time to communicate than you would with a native speaker of English, not only to be polite but also to allow your companions time to formulate their thoughts in a language foreign to them. Although your colleagues may demonstrate good verbal skills, you cannot assume they are processing the information received as quickly or as effectively as you would. By becoming comfortable with silence, you will place your partner at ease. It is also important to be attentive to the nonverbal cues that may be offered, many of which you will not be able to interpret at first. By developing certain communication skills, for example, paraphrasing, repeating back what has been said to you, and looking for or requesting feedback to make sure your message has gotten through accurately, your communication with nonnative English speakers will be enriched. By and large the English skills of the people of Hong Kong are good; verbal communication will not be as crucial in your relation-ship with them as will an understanding of the cultural aspects of communication (see chapters 5 and 6 for information on cultural matters).

5

Doing Business in Hong Kong

Securing and reinvesting profit is the chief dynamic of all Hong Kong business transactions, whether it be developing a joint-venture contract or negotiating a price for household goods and services. Hong Kong was built by the ingenuity and sheer grit of small family entrepreneurs, perhaps starting by hawking a small tray of jewelry on the streets of North Point, then slowly reinvesting their profit and building equity until they were able to buy a store, and finally going on to develop an import-export manufacturing business or a global joint venture. Industrious, quick-thinking, go-getting, patient, and persistent—these are the descriptors of any successful person, Western or Chinese, in Hong Kong. The roots of this aggressiveness, or Hong Kong "ethos," as it is called, are not only the skills and temperament of the people but also the unsettled political-economic conditions that have stimulated the Hong Kong businessperson to concentrate on establishing personal and family stability and security today, in the face of an uncertain future.

THE AGREEMENT

The continuity of a secure business environment in Hong Kong depends on the historic December 1984 agreement to return Hong Kong to China and the confidence of the business community in that agreement. The agreement provides that on July 1, 1997, Hong Kong will return to Chinese sovereignty under self-rule while maintaining its current economic and social infrastructure. Hong Kong will become a Special Administrative Region of China, at least until 2047. During this time it will retain its own treaties, travel documents, and currency. While China will have the right to garrison troops within the region, Hong Kong will retain control over its own police. It will be governed by the Basic Law drafted by China with Hong Kong representatives. It is understandable that in the intervening years the degree of credibility and confidence in this agreement will vary as Beijing and the Hong Kong government continue the discussions needed to accommodate the transfer of power. Anxiety caused either by actual events or demoralizing rumors will understandably fluctuate as Hong Kong shifts from being the quintessential capitalistic center to being a major city of a communist system. The fact that more than one million Hong Kong citizens publicly rallied in opposition to the PRC military's oppressive response to the students in Beijing in 1989 demonstrates Hong Kong's potential volatility in the 1990s. The elections in the summer of 1991 gave the Hong Kong community and business leaders a chance to verbalize their disenchantment with the British government. The low turnout unfortunately dramatized the sense of apathy on the part of Hong Kong toward entering the democratic process. Since they were never educated for democracy under the government of Britain, it is not surprising that democracy sparks little interest, although signs of it are developing. Conducting business in Hong Kong during these years will require a constant monitoring of social, political, and economic currents in Hong Kong and, more important, in the PRC.

BUSINESS RELATIONSHIPS WITH THE CHINESE

Chinese companies in Hong Kong are family-owned corporations with strong centralized control. The goal of a traditional Chinese corporation is to secure the long-term financial stability of the family. Chinese business draws on the family for its capital and its human resources and is concerned less with profit than with establishing and

securing family assets, which in turn are passed on from one generation to the next. Family unity and prosperity, under the direction of the
patriarch (and in some cases a matriarch), is the backbone of the
Chinese entrepreneurial system. Business is based on mutually supportive relationships with the suppliers of goods and services. In
addition to a tendency toward nepotism, Chinese companies gather a
cadre of loyal employees who function as honorary family members.
Through their behavior, they demonstrate fidelity to the company, and
the leaders in turn develop a paternal obligation to the employee.
Decision making is located in the highest levels within these corporations, and executives use a "top down" communication style where
suggestion is understood as direction. Deference is always expected
when dealing with the leadership of these companies; informal behavior is inappropriate.

Just as Hong Kong's business community has maintained a
strong family orientation, it has traditionally stayed out of politics and
government. Some ascribe this behavior to the apolitical nature of the
Chinese economic community as well as to the reluctance of an
emigrant refugee population to be critical of the colonial government
which provided refuge to them. Others believe that the Hong Kong
business community is simply too busy with its own livelihood to
concern itself with politics or social responsibility.

As 1997 approaches, it is likely that political noninvolvement and
apathy will end. Once the British Civil Service departs and the Hong
Kong indigenous civil servants retire, the only major group capable of
administering a functional government will be the indigenous executives of Hong Kong.

As a newcomer, you may not easily gain access into this
structured network. The corporate representatives with whom you
relate will be the sons and daughters, nephews and nieces of the family
founders. They, as you, will have been trained in the major universities
of North America and Europe (predominantly England) and will be
knowledgeable in Western as well as Eastern business practices. They
will form a tightly knit network among themselves. Patience and the
ability to establish solid interpersonal relationships with higher management are essential to success.

The indigenous Chinese corporations of Hong Kong range in

size from major conglomerates to small corporations, some choosing to remain small in order to maintain close personal and family ties within the corporate structure. During the years ahead, the major Chinese conglomerates, with their clear plans for global diversification, will have the power and resources to remain active in the Hong Kong market while their kinship networks manage overseas family interests that will provide a survival infrastructure should conditions in Hong Kong radically deteriorate; in other words, they should have the ability to weather the adjustment to reunification. This elite business core will also very likely become more politically concerned, perhaps seeking an active role in the future administration of Hong Kong. The small Hong Kong companies, on the other hand, do not have the resources or political influence to protect their interests and markets. It is conceivable that the indigenous small business community will reflect greater anxiety concerning the growth and development of Hong Kong after 1997 since it will have far more to lose should the business climate deteriorate.

Numerous major multinational corporations have established regional offices in Hong Kong, staffed by Hong Kong's brightest and best, and they appear, at least on the surface, to be culturally international. Doing business with them has a familiar tone, which, unfortunately, can be deceiving to the unaware business representative. Remember that the overall context of Hong Kong is Chinese and not Occidental. Yes, your Chinese colleague will have excellent taste in Western dress, speak English impeccably, and have a sophisticated eye for the best of imported goods. However, while seemingly westernized, he or she is not British or North American but Chinese, and the subtleties of Chinese culture will prevail in your relationship, which calls for consistent courtesy and vigilance on your part. It is not uncommon for the Chinese personnel in these companies to accommodate to Western customs as a way of easing the difficulties westerners have in adjusting to Chinese social and business etiquette, and they will frequently deny cultural differences. Accept this disavowal as an expression of the age-old politeness of the Chinese to visitors but be attentive when your Chinese colleague indicates how "we Chinese" do something. He or she is attempting to focus your behavior and guide it toward greater cultural congruence.

Visiting Chinese Clients

Shortly after you arrive in Hong Kong, make appointments to introduce yourself to your client group, though before you visit an important potential client, try to secure a proper introduction. This is often accomplished with the help of a go-between in Hong Kong, someone who knows you and who is respected by your prospective client. After an initial meeting, future contacts will depend on your ability to establish a personal and professional relationship. Networking is essential in the Asian business context (see section on networking on pages 59–60).

When you visit clients, be sure to have your business card prepared since every business introduction begins with an exchange of cards. It is customary to have cards printed in English on one side and Chinese on the other. Keep them in your pocket rather than in your briefcase, immediately available to present at the moment of greeting. The importance of the business card is that it gives your name and position, thereby allowing the recipient to place you in a hierarchical status framework. Even though this scrutiny may seem somewhat distasteful to westerners, it is essential to the Asians and allows them to give you proper courtesy and respect. The Chinese painstakingly choose personal names and you should too. Frequently, westerners will have their name transliterated into three Chinese characters which sound similar to the sounds of the westerner's surname as heard by the Asian ear. Usually the first character of the Chinese name reflects the family's clan. Therefore, by accepting a clan name you will have some affiliation with all the Lees or Pangs in Hong Kong. The second and third characters are usually selected to reflect some qualities that are admirable, such as the name Naap Dak, which means "collector of virtue." While many westerners have difficulty identifying with such names, they do have meaning to your Chinese colleagues. Ask a Chinese colleague to assist you in choosing a name, which will not only please the Chinese but also deepen your relationship. When receiving a card, be sure to note the person's name and always refer to that person using the appropriate title of "Mister," "Miss," or "Mrs." The Chinese will maintain formality regarding names until a strong relationship has been established. You should also refer formally to anyone else you meet at a Chinese office or when speaking about a third party.

Decision Making and Negotiating

Business negotiations are a mixture of the pursuit of utilitarian self-interest and the affirmation of complicated alliances. Enter any negotiation prepared, knowing the limits and strengths of your position. Expect your Chinese counterparts to ask a number of indirect questions to feel out your position. Allow time to explore your counterparts' opinions through open-ended questions that permit the disclosure of information while sheltering your opinion. Avoid offensive and direct questions and never place a negotiating partner on the defensive. Seemingly unimportant and irrelevant questions are intended to gather information: an informal question on how you spend your vacations provides your colleague with data on your economic status and social class.

Develop clear and rational presentations concerning your product and services and listen astutely to the company leadership's suggestions and comments. Most importantly, be aware that the Hong Kong Chinese are reluctant to pass up an opportunity; they will attempt to meet you in a true win-win fashion. But if you do not enter well prepared, don't lament if you are not in a winning position.

Networking

Extensive networking will be your most valuable tool for operating in Hong Kong. If you had a predecessor and he or she is still in the territory, use that relationship to its advantage and obtain personal introductions to important people. In lieu of personal introductions, get letters of introduction. Memberships in business associations such as your national Chamber of Commerce are valuable. The United States, Canada, Australia, France, Germany, Korea, Switzerland, India, Japan, Sweden, and the United Kingdom all maintain chambers of commerce in Hong Kong. You may also want to contact the Hong Kong General Chamber of Commerce, the Chinese General Chamber of Commerce, and the Kowloon Chamber of Commerce. Social clubs and the expatriate community itself are fertile ground for networking. Although Hong Kong is an extremely large city, the expatriate community is a small village where people know each other's personal and professional business. This natural network system is an asset since it opens up the opportunity for professional contacts. Yet, it also has its drawbacks, mainly the loss of privacy and the temptation it offers as a retreat from the challenges and opportunities of cross-cultural contact with the Chinese. Two publications are good resources for identifying business networks. The American Chamber of Commerce in Hong Kong publishes "Establishing an Office in Hong Kong," which lists the major business organizations. The Hong Kong Convention and Incentive Travel Bureau publishes a comprehensive booklet entitled "Associations and Societies in Hong Kong," which facilitates the identification of people with similar business interests.

Another area of networking potential is the Chinese staff within your firm or industry. Your employees, both secretarial and managerial, are invaluable not only for gaining information but also for disseminating it, both formally and informally. Through careful team development, you can build strong alliances which will help you achieve your objectives.

CULTURAL IMPLICATIONS

There are major characteristics or themes that can be identified in Chinese culture that need to be considered and understood when one conducts business in Hong Kong.

Group Orientation

Chinese culture emphasizes the importance of the group over the individual. While individualism is basic to Western thought, the relationship to the group or to the society is more central in Chinese thought. A person does not exist in his or her own context but rather as part of a social network which reflects Confucius's concept of the five basic relationships: sovereign-subject, father-son, husband-wife, elder brother-younger brother, friend-friend. While many Western cultures reward individual effort, Chinese culture rewards collaborative endeavors. Behaviors which reflect team spirit or collegial spirit are expected; excessive individualism, aggressive behavior, or ethnocentric chauvinism are perceived as impolite and unprofessional. Companies from the PRC express this collective nature by fostering a strong regional and national identity, while Hong Kong corporations foster a strong allegiance to the company as family.

Personal Relationships

Hong Kong society is built on a network of personal relationships and concurrent obligations, rooted in the values of the Confucian ethic. In this context, one's word takes on more significance than a clearly defined legal document which delineates the details of an agreement. The Chinese often perceive a contract as little more than an agreement to work together, not as a binding covenant. A contract establishes a relationship in which both sides have a commitment to work out the details. Having a relationship with people who are honorable and trustworthy is important to the Chinese. The quality of your product or service is critical since the Chinese are pragmatic people, but equally important is your personal integrity, which the Chinese sense more by intuition than by gathering information about you.

Politeness and Decorum

Working in a Chinese environment demands politeness and decorum. Greetings, manners, and customs are all very important. Maintaining harmony in relationships is paramount. Frequently, instead of answering a question truthfully, the Chinese will give an expatriate the answer he or she thinks the expat wants to hear. This is not seen as lying but rather as a courtesy designed to avoid explicit disagreement or conflict. In sum, maintaining harmony is more important than risking disagreement or discord. Another behavior motivated by this same value is often troublesome to westerners. At times a

Chinese may believe one thing but act in a manner which is incongruous with that internal belief. For example, the Chinese partner of a joint venture may agree to a deadline, knowing all along that it will not be met. The Chinese do not perceive the agreement as a breach of contract or a contract made in bad faith, but rather as a commitment to work together; details can be worked out as events evolve. This is confusing for westerners who value consistency of belief and action. It is not confusing to the Chinese; it is merely another means of maintaining harmony and displaying courtesy. You will need to develop skills in translating surface messages into what is really being said; in other words, learn when yes or maybe mean no. Anger, hostility, and aggressiveness are all counterproductive in Chinese society. Such unseemly outbreaks of emotion cause both your Chinese colleague and you to lose face. Firm, pleasant persistence will yield better results. Concentrate on building relationships with your Chinese colleagues. Exchange information with them. These efforts will increase your influence far more than bluster. And always keep in mind that the agreeable manner of your Chinese colleagues does not necessarily mean they in fact agree with you. It is more likely a way of maintaining a congenial atmosphere while searching collaboratively for common ground.

Status and Face

All cultures bestow status, but the criteria for achieving position in the society differ from culture to culture. In some, class distinctions are determined by birth and carried throughout one's life. In others, status is earned through work and achievement and displayed by a show of wealth or influence. One determines status in Chinese society by examining interpersonal roles. All relationships among Chinese involve a status hierarchy, where one member is perceived and acknowledged as deserving higher status than the other. In egalitarian cultures such as that of the United States, hierarchically defined status is distasteful, and it will be difficult for people from such cultures to accept or even understand it since the concept is foreign to them. The advantage, on the other hand, is that fewer rules are imposed on visitors. Your mistakes are often graciously overlooked because, after all, you are an outsider and just don't know.

A good rule of thumb is to always act in a polite manner and show respect to others, regardless of their status or position. If you are in the lower status position, you can lose face and embarrass a superior and yourself by acting in a way that disregards the superior's status. Likewise, if you have the higher status, you can clearly lose face by acting in a manner which demeans a subordinate.

Face or *min* is a concept that permeates most Asian cultures. As westerners, we are not accustomed to the notion of face, although many Western cultures do recognize the need for individuals to preserve their self-respect and the importance of interpersonal sensitivity, which is usually expressed through politeness and deference. There are two dimensions that are essential in understanding face. On the one hand, face is the personal integrity or honor that a person cultivates in him- or herself and acknowledges and reinforces in others. On the other, face must be personally cultivated through proper action, so that one learns to act in ways that maintain and demonstrate it. Face is also a family matter. Insults may also be directed at the family: "There is a lack of virtue in the past eight generations of your ancestors."

In no way should you ever cause a Chinese colleague to lose face, whether he or she is a peer with whom you are negotiating a joint venture, a secretary who is assisting you with a proposal, or a factory line worker whom you are training. There is always a need to protect the dignity of self and of others. Asians place a great value on allowing others to escape humiliation.

Pragmatically, what does this concern for face and status mean in day-to-day transactions? First, avoid confrontations which will end with someone proven wrong (especially in the presence of others). Avoid asking direct questions which could elicit any admission of wrongdoing or failure to carry out one's responsibility. Be careful about putting people in a corner. Make your meaning clear but avoid a challenge, and always give the other person face-saving opportunities to back away if there is disagreement. In an office situation, for example, you would not ask your secretary, "Did you notify Mr. Pang of our afternoon meeting as I requested?" Instead, you might ask, "Have you been able to reach Mr. Pang concerning our meeting?" This serves both as a question and as a reminder if the person has, in fact, forgotten. Respect office status. Asking a secretary to prepare coffee because it is quicker than asking the *tea amah* (tea maid) clearly confounds the office hierarchy. Furthermore, it insults the secretary, who is asked to act in a lower status role, and possibly insults the tea amah, who may feel that failure to perform her role is a criticism of her. Face must be considered when giving feedback on performance. Although your Chinese staff, when speaking among themselves, may be extremely direct and openly critical of each other and, on occasion, their superiors, they would never criticize someone to his or her face. Also, never criticize office staff members in front of their colleagues; instead, meet with them privately and use clear descriptive terms, flavored with a supportive paternal direction and interest. Remember also to consider face when it is time for formal performance review. Written evaluations and forms with specific behavioral performance objectives are useful tools. It is best to address the issues directly but politely. One-on-one interviews work best.

Frequently, conflict can be resolved by using a third party as a conveyor of negative feedback or as a mediator for conflict resolution. You can give your Chinese support staff face in front of their subordinates by expressing recognition of the unit's efforts and accomplishments. By praising the unit, you are clearly praising the person who supervises or leads the group. Giving praise and recognition to one's employees creates a positive atmosphere where face is supported and personal and corporate endeavors acknowledged.

Face must, then, not only be protected but given as well. This will require constant attention on your part, but the rewards will be commensurate with the effort. Relationships with your superiors and close personal friends require the most monitoring. When you first establish yourself in your office, tactfully explore status patterns with your staff so that you can begin to understand the hidden roles and relationships that will affect your daily life.

WORKERS' RIGHTS

Fairly stringent employment-rights laws protect nonmanagerial staff in Hong Kong, guaranteeing statutory holidays with pay, sick leave, sickness allowance, paid maternity leave, rest days, and seven days' annual leave. Women and young children are protected by many regulations. There is no legal minimum wage; supply and demand determine wage levels. Benefits may also include free medical treatment, subsidized meals, a good-attendance bonus, and transportation to and from work. In many cases a Lunar New Year bonus, which is equal to a month's wages, is included in a benefits package.

Since the 1920s Hong Kong has had a workplace inspection policy as well as laws to maintain safety standards, health, and workers' compensation. Its reputation for implementing and enforcing the International Labor Office Conventions is also outstanding. Overall, there has been little labor conflict. Thus, though trade unions are active in Hong Kong, they have not gained the same power as they have in most Western countries. Other than the strike of the machinery workers in 1920 and the Great Guangzhou-Hong Kong Strike of 1925, Hong Kong has been free from major territory-wide industrial actions. Much of the unions' focus has reflected the political interests of the Communist or Nationalist parties, in a way playing out the historic tensions of twentieth-century China.

OFFICE RELATIONSHIPS

Hong Kong's educational system, which, as noted earlier, is based on memorization, repetition, and the sanctity of the printed word, has had a strong impact on office behavior. It results in an exaggerated reliance on written instructions and prescribed office procedures. The primacy of the teacher in the Chinese educational experience is also transposed to the workplace as an uncritical abdication of responsibility to higher authorities, precluding any possibility that a subordinate would even question a supervisor, much less confront him or her. This boss-is-always-right attitude can be uncomfortable for Western managers with an egalitarian bent or who value getting frank feedback from their subordinates. However, Chinese who have been exposed to Western education, either through university training abroad or through Western-based secondary education in the territory, will be more inclined to take initiative, assume responsibility, and be direct.

Office relationships are largely based on status, as we've discussed earlier, which is reflected in the use of office space. While Chinese clerical and administrative staff are frequently comfortable working together in a common open office space, senior staff want an office, no matter what its size, since it reflects their status within the organization and therefore allows them to maintain face.

Punctuality is valued and indicates respect. Nonetheless, punctuality for meetings is frequently difficult due to traffic congestion. In general, however, the Chinese are energetic workers and will rarely miss deadlines.

Two aspects of office social relationships may surprise the expatriate manager. One is that office staff will frequently date each other, usually associating in group activities prior to more individualized dating. Another is that Chinese businessmen may invite female companions other than their wives to business functions.

Women managers are probably more readily accepted in Hong Kong than elsewhere in Asia because of Hong Kong's long exposure to more egalitarian Western views and also because of the presence of large numbers of well-educated women. While women may not be accepted as equals because of the overriding Confucian ethic which places men in a superior position, Hong Kong women are professional equals and are judged according to their skills and expertise.

Working with Bilingual Staff

While English is one of the official languages of Hong Kong and the major international language for business, Chinese colleagues and contacts may not be fluent speakers. English remains a second language for many professional people and skill levels vary tremendously. To complicate matters further, both American and British English are widely spoken. Your staff may use either (or even a combination of both) system of spelling and pronunciation. And no matter how fluently a Chinese speaks English, it is still wise to avoid idiomatic expressions, sports jargon, and jokes—at least until you know a person well. With the exodus of Hong Kong's brightest entrepreneurial class, some have felt that the standard of English has declined.

BUSINESS MECHANICS

Business Hours

Generally, expatriate staff arrive in the office around 8:30 A.M. and remain until 5:00 P.M. with a lunch break between 1:00 P.M. and 2:00 P.M. Chinese staff, both clerical and administrative, work from 7:30-8:00 A.M. to 5:00-6:00 P.M. Some Chinese business houses open at 10:00 in the morning and close at 8:00 in the evening. Chinese lunches are frequently brought in and are eaten in the lunchroom or sometimes at a desk. Occasionally, Chinese staff may take some additional time to do their shopping. Breaks are a matter of company policy, but most people keep a cup of tea or hot water on their desks. The Hong Kong business community entertains extensively; many routine weekdays are followed by a cocktail or dinner party. It is common to work half days on Saturday (from 9:00 A.M. to 1:00 P.M.). Overtime is generally acceptable unless employees are required to put in long days on a regular basis without remuneration. Part of the reason that office staff arrive early and stay late lies in the difficulty of traveling in Hong Kong because of the heavy traffic and excessive crowds and also because many workers live in overcrowded homes that are not air-conditioned.

Public Holidays

Sundays are observed as holidays by the government and by nearly all business offices. Also observed are the following seventeen public holidays, eleven of which are statutory, requiring employers to give the day off with pay:

First weekday in January
Lunar New Year's Day

Second day of Lunar New Year
Third day of Lunar New Year
Ching Ming Festival
Good Friday
Saturday following Good Friday
Easter Monday
Birthday of Queen Elizabeth
Dragon Boat Festival
First weekday in July
First weekday in August
Liberation Day—Last Monday in August
Day following Chinese Mid-Autumn Festival
Chung Yeung Festival
Christmas Day
First weekday after Christmas Day

Availability of Personnel

Chinese secretarial staff are, as a whole, well trained and experienced. American expatriate wives often work in secretarial positions, but they frequently have restricted schedules based on their spouses' summer-leave policy. There is also a sizable group of British secretarial staff with a reputation for being extremely efficient.

As 1997 approaches, hiring considerations will become increasingly paramount. Large numbers of qualified senior and middle managers have chosen to emigrate at a rate of approximately sixty thousand per year. In addition, more and more of the gifted business personnel who are not invested in Hong Kong companies or who are not tied to Hong Kong for other reasons can be expected to gravitate to global firms to protect their future. By working in international Hong Kong companies with worldwide operations, they hope to secure a place for themselves that will enable them to move elsewhere easily in the event that the future of Hong Kong does not work out the way optimistic sinologists are predicting. Companies will need to offer a variety of substantial benefits to attract and maintain qualified staff during the 1990s as the pool of good candidates for senior- and middle-management positions dwindles. Interestingly, this loss of talented managers in Hong Kong presents a unique opportunity for overseas Chinese who are currently holding international passports to reintegrate themselves into the life of Hong Kong or China. It should also enable expatriates to enter the job market without the fear of displacing a local Chinese, which has been something of a sore point in Hong Kong in the past.

Business Communications and Postal Service

The communications industry is highly developed, as would be expected in any great financial center. A wide range of business services is provided, including telex, telephone, telegram, leased circuits, bureaufax, IDAS (International Database Access Service), and international facsimile. Cable and wireless sales offices provide twenty-four-hour service and are located in Exchange Square in Central and Hermes House in Kowloon, with additional offices in Sheung Wan, Wanchai, Causeway Bay, Mong Kok, Kai Tak Airport, Kwun Tong, Tsuen Wan, and Tuen Mun. Communication services to ships at sea as well as air-to-ground long-range telephone systems, International Direct Dialing, and local and international audio teleconferencing services are all available. DATAPAK, a digital public data network, provides local and international data transmission services. STARLINE provides call waiting, call forwarding, abbreviated dialing appointment service, and do-not-disturb service.

The business and residential community is serviced by over one hundred post offices throughout the territory. Each weekday the main industrial and business centers receive two mail deliveries. Airmail to all major overseas destinations is dispatched daily, and "Speedpost" is available for rapid overseas deliveries.

Taxation

Taxation is based on income from profits in Hong Kong through a trade, profession, or business; salary; property that produces rental income; and interest payments on income from Hong Kong. Tax rates are low, with a standard personal tax rate of 15 percent and a profit tax for companies and unincorporated businesses of 16.5 percent and 15 percent respectively. Expatriates will be subject to the salaries tax only if their visit to Hong Kong exceeds a total of sixty days in the year of assessment. Income for services rendered by a person outside of Hong Kong is not subject to salaries tax. Consult your personal or corporate accountant concerning your tax liability and the particular features of your national tax policy.

Working Dependents

Given the ease of acquiring household help, many expatriate spouses have found Hong Kong to be an excellent place to expand their career interests, develop new skills, and become "a big fish in a small pond." Although these positions often have limited salaries, they provide opportunities to develop careers which will enhance one's resumé for reentry into the work force upon repatriation. Women do not need a work permit and can usually find employment either through agencies or through advertisements in the *South China Morning Post* on Saturdays and the *Hong Kong Standard* on Fridays. Jobs for teenage children are rare, even baby-sitting, because of the common practice of having household help who take care of children.

Business Centers and Temporary Office Space

Many major hotels as well as twenty individual business centers provide full office services to the occasional visitor or the business-person seeking temporary administrative support. Secretarial, translating, copying and printing, and word processing services are all available. Prices vary from hotel to hotel. The American Chamber of Commerce offers limited rentals of offices and conference space. Consult the Yellow Pages for additional services through Hong Kong's business district. Some accounting and legal services list a private address as well as an answering service and forwarding assistance.

DOING BUSINESS IN THE SHENZHEN ECONOMIC ZONE

Shenzhen, a new industrial city located in Guangzhou Province and developed by the People's Republic of China as part of its current plan to establish economic zones, is attracting international investments because of low labor costs and minimal taxation. Ten years ago this city was a small village adjacent to the Hong Kong border, but today it is an integral part of a developing industrial corridor linking Hong Kong as a port and financial center with the interior of China, as the site of low-cost manufacturing. But many people are skeptical of Shenzhen's ability to live up to its promise of constructing eighty-story office towers and thirty-story factories. Corruption and lax work habits have hampered the efforts of some firms attempting to set up there. The Chinese government's insistence that all goods be exported is also a drawback. Nevertheless, since Shenzhen is one of the few places in the People's Republic where foreign-owned corporations can build factories with Chinese labor and where no Chinese partner is required, this community will most likely continue to be of interest to the international community. Predictions of its success and the rate at which it will grow vary dramatically. Size estimates range from two to three million people by the turn of the century.

Travel to the Shenzhen Special Economic Zone is relatively easy. Double-decker buses and air-conditioned coaches are available through Citybus (China) Ltd., which also offers tours, lunch included. Or you can take the Kowloon-Canton Railway, crossing the border to China at the Lo Wu Bridge, then take a coach or taxi to your specific destination. The Miramar Hotel in Hong Kong has a chauffeur-driven service to Shenzhen and Shekou. Finally, Hovercraft service to Shenzhen departs from Kowloon's Taikoktsui Ferry Pier or the Macao Ferry Terminal several times a day.

DOING BUSINESS WITH THE EXPATRIATE
COMMUNITY OF HONG KONG

The British

While Americans make up the largest group of westerners in Hong Kong, special attention must of course be given to the British presence in the territory.

The original principal trading houses of Hong Kong were staffed by the British—and still are, though to a lesser degree. With the expansion of the colonial government, great numbers of British came to Hong Kong to work in the infrastructure of this Victorian enclave, filling posts in the civil bureaucracy, military, schools, hospitals, and churches. Enterprising British traders and their families created a colonial society that valued permanence, tradition, individualism, self-reliance, and self-control. Status has always been important to the British, who are very sensitive to indications of class, such as regional accents and academic credentials. While life in Hong Kong is less stratified than in the United Kingdom, class structure continues to be influential, perhaps most keenly felt in the sharp division between the British business community and the now dwindling British military and police establishments.

In doing business with the British, you will need to accommodate to their corporate culture. Schedules and promptness are important, so make an appointment as far in advance as possible and do your best (allowing extra time for the proverbial traffic congestion) to arrive on time or a bit early. If your lead time is short, however, the British will make every effort to accommodate your schedule. When you arrive at an office, you will probably be introduced by the secretary. A firm handshake is in order, followed by introductory conversation or chit-chat on the weather, a sailing race, or some other sporting event. Given the British propensity for formality and good manners, it is wise to wait for your British host to initiate the use of first names. Titles are also valued, so if you are dealing with a "Sir," be sure to use his title. Once the preliminaries are concluded, proceed to the business at hand. Your host is interested in your proposal, not your personal affairs. This relatively formal behavior is in sharp distinction to the informal style frequently associated with American business behavior and to the relationship building valued by the Chinese. When your business has been completed, it is up to you to initiate your departure; the British consider it impolite to dismiss visitors. Your host will then walk you to the door and see you out. If you attend a dinner with British colleagues, you will find their sense of formality extends to the dinner table as well, where seating arrangements will indicate status and position. Business is not discussed over dinner as it often is among Americans but is saved for the office or conference room.

In negotiations, the British will not prevaricate, but neither will they reveal the whole truth. On reaching an agreement, a handshake and oral approval are considered morally binding. A written and legal document is merely a confirmation of the agreement that has already been reached. The Chinese also value verbal contracts. Both these styles clearly vary from the litigiousness of Americans.

While the British are loyal to their employers and consider job-hopping a sign of flightiness or unreliability, their identity is not tied to their association with a corporation or organization. One's identity is derived from one's own values and self-image. Identification is first with family, then community, region, and nation. Business acquaintances and personal friends are kept distinct.

The Americans

Hong Kong has maintained a strong economic relationship with the United States, both countries exchanging goods freely. Since Hong Kong is a customs-free port, no import duty is placed on exports from the United States. The U.S. is also a major importer of goods from Hong Kong. The U.S. government maintains the largest of its consular offices in Hong Kong, serving well over 16,500 U.S. citizens. As noted earlier, U.S. expatriates currently outnumber all other expatriate groups; consequently, their informal corporate culture is well established. Some Chinese like to contrast the Americans with the British, who, rightly or wrongly, are labeled "colonizers." Nevertheless, the American and British expatriate communities have a lot in common and individuals often establish a great deal of rapport with each other. At Hong Kong parties it is not unusual to hear British and American friends avidly discussing regional and global politics as one might hear cousins discussing family matters.

6

Customs and Courtesies

CHINESE VALUES

Hong Kong's high-tech cosmopolitanism contrasts sharply with many of the traditional values that the expatriate will observe among the Chinese. These values are rooted in Buddhism, Confucianism, and Taoism. Although somewhat blurred over the centuries, these basic philosophies are the foundation of the Chinese values of family, harmony, the balancing of good and evil, and the meaning of life and death.

The Chinese Family

The family is the key to understanding Chinese culture. When China was predominantly an agricultural society, the cornerstone of the family was the ancestral home, where it was common to have three or four generations living in the same household. Given the small size of the lodgings in which most Hong Kong Chinese live today, it is difficult to imagine a small nuclear family, much less an extended family, living in such close quarters. Yet, extended-family living continues because the value of the family remains strong, and the interlocking roles and responsibilities of each member support closely knit family groups. In most Western cultures the major family unit is the husband-wife dyad;

in Chinese family structure, this bond is secondary to the parent-child relationship. Family, in the Chinese context, consists of all generations and includes not only extended-family members who are living but those members from the past and into the future as well.

Since family structure is so important to the maintenance of cultural values of the Hong Kong Chinese, it is not surprising that births, weddings, and deaths take on a particular significance. Each of these events insures the family lineage will continue and maintains the centuries-old connections between ancestors, the living, and the future family members. Each family member has obligations and responsibilities which cannot be denied or ignored.

Births. Births are happy occasions since they guarantee the continuity of the lineage of the paternal clan. Traditionally, mother and child were secluded during the first month after the baby is born. It was thought that if anyone other than a close relative saw the child, the baby might be seriously frightened or become ill. A special soup is still prepared for the mother, consisting of hard-boiled eggs and pigs feet boiled in vinegar and laced with large amounts of fresh ginger. This blend is supposedly a health aid for the mother, but it is also considered a treat and is offered to family and close friends and neighbors. Chinese women do not conduct any celebrations prior to the birth of the child as do Western women with their baby showers. A banquet, called *mun yuht* or "full month," is held at the end of the first month, and all of the family and important friends are invited. It is on this occasion that the child's name is given. If you are invited to such a banquet, a small gift of money in a *lai see* packet (red gift envelope) or small children's toy from your country would be in order.

Weddings. Marriage requires two ceremonies: one at the city hall or one of the authorized churches in Hong Kong and the other at the Chinese marriage banquet that evening. Either of these ceremonies may be quite Western, including a white wedding dress. If the wedding is in a church, you may be invited, but more than likely, you will only be invited to the evening Chinese wedding banquet. Only immediate family attends the civil ceremony at city hall.

The evening banquet is the occasion for the traditional Chinese wedding, where the bride wears an elaborate red wedding dress. The marriage, according to Chinese custom, is sealed when the bride serves tea to the senior female of her husband's family. Through this token of respect to the senior woman of the family and that woman's reciprocal acceptance of this youngest clanswoman's deference, the bride is accepted into the groom's family. Large numbers of friends and acquaintances are invited to this banquet. The traditional wedding gift is money or a gift certificate presented in a special red envelope, which can be purchased at local stores. The sum of money should cover the cost of your banquet meal plus some additional gift money. The amount must be in even denominations since odd numbers are considered bad luck.

Funerals. Death is honored by a public wake and a private funeral service and burial. During your stay in Hong Kong you may at times need to attend the wake of a staff member's parent. Your attendance will be highly valued and will give both you and your staff member face. Throughout Hong Kong you will find funeral homes where wakes are held for the deceased. During the wake the coffin (made of wooden planks and assembled to look like a hollow tree) is placed in the visiting hall along with a picture of the deceased as well as the ancestral tablet bearing the name and date of birth of the deceased. The family of the deceased sits to one side of the coffin area. As a visitor, you should pay your respects by standing in front of the coffin and making three reverential bows. After this, offer some words of consolation to the family. In expressing condolences, avoid any reference to the death itself or any associated illness; instead, offer your assistance to the family. It is appropriate to send a floral arrangement, and you will always find a number of floral shops specializing in funeral wreaths near the funeral homes. White chrysanthemums are the traditional funeral flower (never bring white flowers into anyone's home, since white is used only for mourning in Hong Kong as it is throughout Asia). In some cases, there may be a fund for the benefit of the family. If you contribute, in this case give an *uneven* amount, since odd numbers are associated with sadness. If the family is very traditional, family members will wear white clothes, usually hemp, during the funeral and burial services. Chinese custom requires a prescribed period of public mourning. During this time women wear black while men wear only a small piece of black cloth, approximately one by two inches, attached to their clothing. Some women wear a small woolen white flower in their hair for the death of a parent and a blue flower for the death of a sibling.

Funeral services, attended only by the family, are conducted in the funeral halls and can be extremely noisy, with music and chanting. Some Chinese may include a Christian church service, but, more commonly, memorial church services are conducted at a later date. Following the service is the interment of the deceased in the cemetery, again with only the family. Since land is very limited, cremation is a frequent alternative to burial. Persons interred in the ground remain there for seven years, after which time the remains are exhumed and the bones scraped and cleaned (traditionally by the youngest woman in the clan) and then reinterred in small bone boxes within a smaller plot. During burial ceremonies, filial respect is frequently shown by an extreme show of emotion and, at times, argumentation. A classic example is the argument that often occurs among brothers as to the position of the casket during interment. The apparent conflicts are, in reality, only a demonstration of respect for the deceased. Gravesites vary from the multitiered, mountainside cemeteries on Hong Kong Island (with individual sites) to tightly sealed burial urns (placed on a solitary hillside overlooking ocean inlets) to a field of large mausoleum-type structures shaped like semicircular courtyards. All burial sites and ceremonies and the people attending them are shown great respect. Taking photographs at too close a range interrupts a very private matter and thus is disrespectful.

A word of caution is needed when communicating with the Chinese concerning death or severe illness. One does not refer to death directly. A common euphemism for dying is that the person has "gone over the mountain," which is similar to saying that someone has "passed on." To speak of death or any unhappy event is, in traditional belief, to call these unlucky and unhappy forces into play within one's own life. Consequently, avoid such unpleasant themes at all cost.

Respect for Ancestors

Contrary to what many westerners believe, the Chinese do not worship their ancestors. In fact their religious tradition does not even include the concept of worship as Western Christians understand the term. Demonstrating respect for one's ancestors is, however, highly valued. The current generation has an obligation to respect all its ancestors. Most homes have a small ancestral shrine containing the family ancestral tablets. In some homes, fruit and incense are placed on the shrine. Two holidays are dedicated to honoring one's ancestors. One is Ching Ming, which is celebrated on the 106th day after the winter solstice, usually occurring in early April. On this day most members of the family visit the graves of their ancestors, provided there are family gravesites in Hong Kong. Some local families visit temples where their family tablets are enshrined and where either Buddhist or Taoist rites are carried out on their behalf. On this holiday families sweep and clean the graves and arrange fresh flowers. They bring food to be offered to the ancestors, which is later shared, in a picnic style, among the family there at the gravesites. Ching Ming is a day of respect and remembrance of one's ancestors; yet, it is also a family holiday. Don't plan to travel to the New Territories on this day since the roads are extraordinarily congested.

The second day of respect is Chung Yeung, which is observed on the ninth day of the ninth month (October). This occasion commemorates a Han Dynasty soothsayer's warning of impending danger. The soothsayer counseled a man to lead his family to higher ground to avoid disaster. By saving his family, he was able to perpetuate his ancestors. The obligatory hike to the cemetery or in some cases just up a mountain honors this event and brings luck to the family.

Respect for Older People

The emphasis on family, including the respect of children for their parents, naturally leads to the notion of respect by the Chinese community for its senior members. Older persons are always treated with deference. Respect for elders is not only a clear extension of the Confucian parent-child relationship but also a recognition by the younger generation of their gratitude, respect, and love for those who have aided in their development. Throughout China's history the elderly have traditionally been cared for by their relatives. Nothing has changed much even now. Although some Buddhist associations and several religious groups have residential care facilities for the elderly, these resources are very limited; care for dependent elders still falls to the family.

You should be courteous to the elderly in any situation. Greet them first and bow politely. You may note that older people will clasp their own hands and shake them rather than shaking your hand. When meeting with a group of elderly persons, greet each in the order of their seniority. Hold doors for them, do not sit in their presence unless invited to, avoid keeping them waiting, and offer them every courtesy. Give them time to lead the conversation and don't interrupt. Talk around a point if you must disagree, but never contradict or correct them openly.

Child Rearing

You will probably notice an interesting discrepancy between respect for older persons and an extremely relaxed, permissive attitude toward young children, especially those four years or younger. Children are highly valued in Chinese families—after all, these small sons carry forward the family line and these small daughters are the "gold" who will produce future generations. Small children are much loved. They are indulged, catered to, and not disciplined during their first four years. Once they begin school, however, the years of freedom are abruptly ended. Suddenly, parents begin to scold their children freely and the children must learn to take a subordinate role within the disciplined and structured family system. The youngest is now the bottom of the family ladder. Each child, frequently known by the number of his or her birth order, has a unique family responsibility, which usually falls most heavily on the oldest son and/or daughter.

Relationships between Men and Women

Custom prescribes the role of women as wives and mothers, subservient to their husbands. The wife, however, has wide latitude to exercise personal power in the home. Customarily, she manages the family finances and often maintains her own independent bank accounts. Frequently she retains her maiden name. But women also have traditionally functioned as laborers in Chinese society. Since many Hong Kong families trace their origins to the farming communities of Guangzhou, older Hong Kong women are accustomed to hard work. The Hakka women, with their wide woven hats, work as hard as male laborers in construction and in the factories. Other women apply themselves diligently to piecework in their homes.

The role of Chinese women in Hong Kong is evolving under the impact of increased educational opportunities and other changes. More and more women are moving into leadership positions at all levels of government and business. A woman who is an entrepreneur is respected for her skills and abilities, as she would be in any world-class city. Hong Kong women lead other Asian women in their personal and professional freedom and are clearly more advanced than in Taiwan and frequently more accomplished than their social counterparts in the PRC.

Social relationships among young men and women are more stylized and formal than they are in the West. Modern young couples date and select their marriage partners, but dating is still circumscribed. Older adolescents and college students tend to go out in groups rather than in couples. Although touching between members of the opposite sex in public is not as taboo in Hong Kong as in other Asian countries, it is not condoned either. A Western woman should not hug or kiss a Chinese man she considers a good friend, nor should a Western man kiss a Chinese female friend. Many Chinese women are unfamiliar with the Western custom whereby a man holds a door open, adjusts her chair, or holds her coat. Women who have been exposed to Western customs more easily accept these behaviors than other Chinese women, who may feel awkward with such attention.

If touching among members of the opposite sex is discouraged, among people of the same sex it is quite acceptable. If you are a young woman, you may find a Chinese female friend taking your hand as you walk down the street. This is a familiar sight in Europe and Latin America as well. In Southeast Asian countries, men often hold hands in public, which demonstrates a close friendship but does not convey any sexual messages.

Many people from European and North and South American cultures instinctively touch people at various times and are unaware that this style of closeness and proximity is uncomfortable for Asians. They nudge a friend over a joke, poke someone to give emphasis to a point, take a person's arm when crossing the street, throw an arm across a shoulder to indicate warmth, display friendly feelings, and readily kiss family and close friends of the opposite or same sex to say hello or good-bye. You must be diligent in avoiding any personal touching while you are in Hong Kong and the rest of Asia. People, particularly in rural areas, may want to touch you, however, out of curiosity. If either you or your children are blonde, you will be of particular interest, and people may want to touch your skin and your hair. Have the grace and humor to accept such inquisitiveness.

FUNG SHUI

Fung shui, literally meaning "wind, water," is the practice of geomancy, which is based on a belief that luck is related to the balancing of the forces of heaven and earth (the yin and yang and the five elements of water, fire, wood, metal, and air) with the forces within individuals and families. The fung shui man, by using a compass centered in a circular wooden board engraved with the signs of the zodiac and other neo-Confucian cosmological signs, sites proper locations for buildings, graves, windows, and exits and entrances. He also calculates the most propitious time for a variety of events, including ground breakings or contract signings. For some believers, positioning a building on a hill properly is important; if the hill is considered to be a sleeping dragon, for instance, it would not be comfortable if some edifice were placed on its tail or some tender part of its body. The consequence of poor fung shui is bad luck, and Hong Kong is replete with stories about the influence of fung shui. Sit, for example, in the lobby of the Regent Hotel and enjoy the hotel lobby's view of the harbor, but be thankful for the geomancer who encouraged the architects to place the forty-foot lengths of glass in the first floor lobby so that "the dragons" can still pass through the building to enter the harbor in the place where they like to take their baths. A major bank positioned its entrances on the diagonal of the street intersection so that it would maintain good fung shui. Stories also abound of people who ignored fung shui and paid for it. Is fung shui superstition or reality? Each expatriate must come to a personal decision, but respect is due to those who take this custom seriously, whether they be the CEO of a company or the tea amah.

Note the number of octagonal mirrors or deflectors that are hung outside the windows of Hong Kong apartments and buildings. The purpose of these *bat gwa* is to confuse the unlucky spirit that may be heading your way and deflect it. The presence of bat gwa in a window signals that the people inside may still believe in or honor fung shui.

CHINESE EATING CUSTOMS AND MANNERS

People in Hong Kong eat frequently—breakfast, lunch, afternoon snack or tea, dinner, and evening snack. When all meals are taken at home, the family cook (usually the wife) is busy throughout the day. Fortunately, they also eat out a lot. Local restaurants are inexpensive, and westerners generally find that with the exception of some of the street stalls, most are clean and serve good food. Outside of Central and the tourist areas of Kowloon it may be difficult to secure an English menu, but there is always someone to help. There are two basic styles of eating Chinese food: family style and banquet style.

Family Style

Family-style meals, as in most cultures, are fairly informal and relaxed. Some of the customs will be familiar to those who have dined at a Chinese restaurant; some will not. Along with the rest of the meal, you will be served a bowl of rice and given a pair of chopsticks and a Chinese-style spoon. Tea will be served in small traditional cups or plain drinking glasses. When you are eating in a restaurant, the host or head of the household will order the meal for everyone and will signal when to begin eating. Courses are brought to the table at the same time and placed in the middle of the table. As a rule of thumb, a dish is ordered for each person seated at the table, plus a soup. It is appropriate to have several bowls of rice during a family meal.

All dishes are shared, requiring each person to select food from the common dish. Never eat directly out of the serving dish, although you don't need to actually transfer the food to your plate either. What you can do is take a portion in your chopsticks from the serving dish, touch or pause over the rice, and then put it in your mouth. Touching or pausing over the rice breaks the motion so that it is not considered eating from the serving dish. Avoid stacking a large amount of food on your plate or in your bowl at any one time. When taking food from the serving dishes, take only portions that are on the platter closest to you, and never pick food from the most distant part of a platter or choose the best pieces. In restaurants, platters are placed on lazy Susans for easy access to all the dishes. During informal meals, platters will be passed around the table. Your host will usually encourage you to eat more than you would wish. Accept this custom as your host's way of showing you respect. Leave the last pieces of food on a serving dish, signifying that the host has ordered sufficient food. If your host offers you the last portion, accept it graciously. If you notice that someone is serving you food with their chopsticks, don't be alarmed. Look carefully, and you will see that the chopsticks have been reversed. Drinks are usually not served with a meal, but brandy is often offered prior to the beginning of the meal. At informal meals, people drink beer.

Depending on how informal your Chinese companions are, you may observe two methods for negotiating bones in meats and fish. Many meat dishes are cut in a manner which retains the meat on the bones. The small piece of meat (and bone) is placed in one's mouth and the meat removed with the teeth. Depending on class and custom, the bones may be lowered discreetly with chopsticks or dropped from the mouth on the table. The Chinese do not spit bones on tables but rather lower their heads to dispose of the unwanted bones. And don't worry about the amount of drippings or rice spilled on the table; no one will care. Both men and women use toothpicks, but they always use the left hand to cover the mouth so that others are not observing an open mouth or teeth.

The meal will end with a bowl of soup, which is put into your by-now-emptied rice bowl although sometimes a clean bowl may be provided. Desserts are not common in the Western sense of cakes and sweets, but there is often a variety of fruit and custard dishes.

When you are in a restaurant and your supply of tea has run out, lift the lid of the teapot and balance it on top of the pot. This signals to the waiter that you need more tea. The Chinese rarely drink coffee with meals, reserving it for breakfast or evening snack, and usually serving it heavily laced with sugar and milk.

Rarely will you experience a family-style meal in a home. Homes in Hong Kong are extremely small and, outside of the upper-middle class and wealthy, most entertaining is done in restaurants.

Banquet Style

Banquets are quite different from informal dinners and deserve some additional explanation. Shortly after your arrival in Hong Kong, you will be honored by your Chinese staff or will have to entertain business associates at a banquet. Chinese banquet tables are usually round, and the place of honor is not at the customary head of the table but rather at the seat facing the door. Seats to the left and right of the guest of honor are of highest status. Your host and/or hostess will sit at the side of the table most convenient for serving and closest to the door.

Traditional banquets have at least twelve dishes, starting with four cold dishes which are considered appetizers. These are followed by four quick-sautéd dishes, followed by four main-course dishes. The end of the banquet is marked by the arrival of two soups, one thick and one thin. A dessert consisting of a sweet soup and often a kind of sticky rice and fruit concoction completes the meal. If you are in a restaurant, portions of each dish will initially be served by a waiter; if you are in a private home, by the host or hostess. Dining utensils will be changed frequently. No starch staple will be served until just before the sweet soup, when some rice or sauteed noodles will appear. It is not polite to finish these bowls of rice or noodles since the implication would be that the meal was inadequate.

You are expected to eat only a little of each of the many dishes that are served despite the fact that, if your host or hostess is attending you, he or she will delight in piling your dish with more food than you care to consume. There is a little ritual involved in saying no. The first time you say it, your host will continue to place food on the plate. When your host insists again that you eat, again say no but add some kind words concerning the generosity of the host. The host will continue again to serve you but generally after the third no, the host accepts that the guest is satisfied.

Restaurants

Hong Kong offers the unique opportunity to sample almost all varieties of one of the greatest of all cuisines, Chinese. There are more than six thousand Chinese restaurants from which to choose. Due to the location and demographic makeup of Hong Kong, the predominant cuisine is Cantonese, but the cuisines of Shanghai, Chiu Chow, Hakka, Szechuwan, and northern China are also represented. Equally enticing is the variety of other Asian restaurants—Vietnamese, Indonesian, Japanese, Korean, Thai, Filipino, Indian, Burmese, Sri Lankan, and Straits Malay. And for those with Continental preferences, major Hong Kong hotels feature German, Swiss, Austrian, British, Italian, and American cuisine. British- or Australian-style pubs are good places for a quick lunch and a pleasant evening drink with friends. In addition there are a number of private clubs, many of which are national associations, offering luncheon and catering facilities. For long-term Hong Kong residents, these clubs are popular, but they have waiting lists for joining and most require quite substantial membership fees. Lastly, Hong Kong has a wide range of fast-food restaurants ranging from the street-side Chinese food stands, *dai-pai-dongs,* to the Western food franchises.

Chinese Food

Eating is an essential part of any culture, but the Chinese have refined it to an art. You will want to quickly become familiar with and knowledgeable about the regional cuisines. The Chinese are so enamored of food that a common Hong Kong greeting is, " Where is your home village?" The answer is both a clue to the person's ancestral roots and an identification of the style of "home cooking." Another standard greeting is the English equivalent of "Have you eaten?" again expressing an overriding involvement in food and eating. To help you on your way to learning about Chinese cuisines, we offer the following brief descriptions of the four main regional foods.

Southern China. Cantonese or southern cuisine is "the" cuisine of Hong Kong since the majority of the people are from Guangdong Province. The majority of Chinese residing in the Chinatowns of North America and the United Kingdom are also Cantonese. Therefore, westerners frequently recognize this style, although their hometown version has been so adulterated that westerners arriving in Hong Kong are pleasantly surprised with how different and better-tasting real Cantonese food is.

Guangdong's Pearl River basin, with its abundance of fish as well as the rich farmland, produces fresh products all year round. This gives the Cantonese the luxury of using pure, fresh ingredients in their dishes. Cantonese chefs concentrate on the texture of foods and excel at sealing in their flavors by cooking them fast at high heat. They use less oil than other regions and prefer to steam or boil many of their foods. They use ginger, garlic, and other spices sparingly; thus the flavors are delicate. Westerners who are used to strongly seasoned Chinese foods frequently have difficulty adjusting to the delicate flavors and textures for which the Cantonese are famous and will frequently overload dishes with soy sauce or some other table spice to compensate for the way they "know Chinese food should taste." Such behavior may easily insult your Cantonese host. Contrary to popular belief, sweet and sour dishes are, in fact, rare among the Cantonese. The development of this dish is generally accepted as an accommodation to Western tastes.

Rice is the principal staple eaten at all meals. Cantonese specialties include roast pork, steamed fish, sliced beef with oyster sauce, clear mushroom soup, minced chicken with corn soup, shark's fin soup, chicken and abalone, stuffed crab claw, steamed chicken with chopped ginger and scallions, lemon chicken, and a wide range of vegetarian dishes. Some oddities include goose and duck feet, sea cucumbers, and dog stew, which is officially banned in Hong Kong but can be purchased in selected markets.

A special treat is *dim sum,* a traditional meal reported to date back to the tenth century. A unique alternative to lunch, dim sum consists of a variety of small, bite-sized delicacies, such as minced pork or prawns wrapped in paper-thin pastry skins, steamed fried rice in lotus-leaf wrapping, spareribs with red pepper sauce, chicken feet stewed in an anise-flavored sauce, and steamed breads stuffed with Cantonese roast pork. Dim sum desserts include crisp and sticky sweet cake topped with almonds, coconut snowballs, and hot custard tart. The meal is accompanied by your choice of a variety of green, black, and semifermented teas.

Beside the foods themselves, dim sum is a social tradition in its own right. Rarely do the Cantonese eat alone. Large groups of people, numbering from six to twelve, crowd around circular tables to share a communal meal, especially on Sunday mornings, when most family groups gather to share food and conversation. During the week, when coworkers gather for lunch, they either adjourn to a local restaurant or have dim sum and other fried dishes delivered to the office.

Almost as if in a Brueghel painting, life surrounds you in the restaurant as the waiters and waitresses hawk their goods, carrying their small trays or pushing their carts, calling each item out by name. Their voices carry from one end of the room to the other as their eyes remain alert to the gestures of the customers who call them to their tables. People select and choose the dishes they want, which are served in lots of two to four small items per dish. Don't be reluctant to ask the waiters to show you the dishes they are hawking. They will enjoy sharing an explanation of the dish with you even if they don't speak your language. At the end of the meal, a waiter prepares your bill by counting up the dishes left on the table, all coded by size and shape. The cost of dim sum is reasonable. If you need a quiet lunch, you can select a restaurant where the dim sum service is sedate.

Be sure to offer yourself and your family the treat of enjoying dim sum in a restaurant which is not frequented by expatriates. Securing a table in such restaurants is usually a feat in itself, but there is a method to it. Walk through the restaurant and find a table which, though occupied, is strewn with empty dishes. Then stand close by while the people finish their last pot of tea. You are clearly staking out your claim. Be patient; eventually the people will leave. Don't be surprised if when you have nearly finished your dim sum, a group of people similarly surround your table. Don't feel rushed; enjoy your tea and then ask for your check. *Guide to Dim Sum Delights*, published by the Hong Kong Tourist Association, is an illustrated guide to a number of easily accessible and good quality dim sum restaurants.

Eastern China. The cuisine of eastern China includes the cuisines of the great cities of Shanghai, Suzhou, Hangzhou and Nanjing. This region, known for its streams, lakes, and canals as well as coastal waters, uses freshwater fish and seafood to create its specialties. A hairy crab, in season only during autumn, is a popular delicacy. Because this region is famous for its concentration of artists, writers, and poets, it seems quite natural that gastronomy has also been traditionally considered an art as chefs competed to reach new heights in taste, shape, and texture. General meat preferences are duck, chicken, and pork. The areas to the south of the Yangtze River provide a wide range of vegetables in season. The food in general is a little oilier than Cantonese and does not rely on mixing foods with sauces; rather, it relies on steaming and stewing. Specialties include meats stewed in soy and anise stocks such as Hangzhou's soy duck or "drunken chicken" (a delicious chicken dish marinated in Chinese wine for one to four days after which it is steamed and then served cold, often as an appetizer), Shanghai ham and crab with special Tientsin cabbage, and a variety of cold appetizers.

Western China. Food from Szechwan and Hunan reflects the ecology of western China. Approximately a thousand miles up the Yangtze River and surrounded by mountains, this very warm and humid area developed a hot and spicy style of food, the spices acting as a preservative as well as inducing sweat to balance the *chi* of the body. One of the favorite flavorings is hot chili oil mixed with fermented black beans. Actually, red chili was introduced only about one hundred years ago. Before that time the region used a fragrant brown peppercorn (cardamom) in combination with other strong spices. Some dishes to try include prawns cooked with chili and garlic, bean curd with minced ground beef and hot bean paste, chili-hot kidneys, Szechwan hot pot, hot and sour soup, and camphor- and tea-smoked duck.

Northern China. Northern Chinese (Beijing) cooking tends to be drier and coarser than food from other regions. Northern chefs prefer to use strong basic flavors such as garlic and ginger. Beijing cuisine includes a good many dishes featuring lamb or mutton because of the influence of the northern sheep herders who live within the borders of Inner Mongolia. Mutton is not usually appreciated by most Chinese. Since the weather in northern China does not support the growth of vegetables outside its short summer growing season, the northern Chinese have traditionally used a great deal of pickled cabbages and cucumbers which are preserved through the winter. Cabbage is the staple winter vegetable, harvested in the fall and buried in pits to preserve freshness. Wheat, not rice, is the starch of this region, supplemented by sorghum, millet, and even sweet potatoes. The cuisine therefore includes many noodle dishes and steamed and baked dumplings and breads. Specialties include the famous Peking roast duck (the taste lies in the skin rather than the meat) served with wheat pancakes, accented with scallions and sweet bean paste sauce. Dumplings are the other northern treasure—made of minced pork seasoned with ginger, garlic, scallions, and cabbage wrapped in pastry skins to form crescent-shaped dumplings which are either steamed, boiled, or fried. Serious diners can manage to eat as many as forty or fifty of these dumplings at a sitting, washed down with steaming bowls of soup. Wrapping the dumplings is an art in itself, with dozens of variations.

During the short winter season in Hong Kong be sure to try a Mongolian fire pot. A boiling caldron of water is brought to your table, accompanied by platters of thinly sliced uncooked meats, vegetables, and noodles. Each diner cooks his own meal. It is similar to Western fondue, the major difference being that the cooking stock is water, which retains the natural flavors of the ingredients. The cooked morsels are then dipped in sauce and eaten. By the end of the meal, the boiling stock has become a rather pleasant soup, which is shared by everyone.

Nightclubs

Nightlife in Hong Kong is exciting and varied. The unsavory reputation of Hong Kong as "girlie bar" heaven, reminiscent of the R & R days of the United States Seventh Fleet during the Vietnam War years, is unfounded. The territory has a spectrum of quite respectable evening entertainment. Most business entertaining involving the Chinese is conducted in the evening and outside the home since the Chinese do not customarily entertain in their homes. The principal hotels of Hong Kong have dinner shows featuring major international performers while Chinese nightclubs provide entertainment ranging from the most current Chinese pop performers of Hong Kong and Taiwan to the traditional classical dancers and singers of mainland China. It is not uncommon for both Western and Chinese couples to entertain their guests in such a manner. Disco clubs as well as British and Australian pubs and Japanese karaoke bars are possibly more attractive venues for younger and singles groups. Hostess clubs offer music, dancing, and companionship, but caution should be taken at these clubs; a sizeable bill can be generated very quickly.

Drinking

In a city that is world famous for having the highest consumption of brandy, it may be hard to believe that the major drink of choice is tea. It is true, nonetheless. There are many varieties of tea, and an excellent way to learn about them is to visit one of the larger stores that sells them.

Beer is also a popular choice to accompany ordinary meals. The locally brewed beers are San Miguel and Carlsberg, and the major imported beer is Tsingtao from Shanghai. China does not have a strong tradition of grape wines although some have recently been introduced. Traditional Chinese rice wines are available and vary in quality. However, be careful when drinking them since they can be quite deceiving to the unaccustomed drinker. The notorious Mau T'ai, used in the PRC, should be sampled in moderation since it often results in a heavy hangover for the apprentice sinophile. (This usually is not a problem since its taste and smell are quite strong and are often unappealing to the uninitiated.)

Drinking Etiquette at Banquets

Unlike family-style meals, where drinks are not usually served with dinner, the use of alcoholic beverages during banquets and formal occasions is customary and has its own etiquette. The Western practice of cocktails before dinner is not a general custom. Unlike family dinners, at which people sip their drinks pretty much as they please, drinking at banquets is highly formalized. Chinese etiquette requires that whenever you take a sip of your brandy or Chinese rice wine, you toast someone, at least at the beginning of the banquet. If you are the guest of honor, you should stand up very early in the banquet and toast your host, thanking him for the delicious meal. He will respond with some disavowal and then toast your virtues as a friend or business associate. After that toast, you can suggest that you and he *yam sing* (bottoms up). Everyone at the banquet usually has an opportunity to propose a toast. Sometimes a whole table of guests will drink to each toast, not just the two people involved.

Chinese men will insist on toasting and usually expect the same of foreign men. Here, the best policy is to sip slowly; otherwise, you may not make it through the entire meal with any semblance of dignity. Chinese women in general will drink considerably less, if at all. Some traditional Chinese have on occasion taken offense at Western women drinking publicly. Frequently, Chinese women will choose fruit juices.

Cultural Differences at the Dining Table

Some general tips on table etiquette will help you put your best foot forward at a Chinese dinner. Correct eating etiquette and adequate skills in using Chinese utensils will signal a cultural appreciation of Chinese customs and a respect for your Chinese hosts. First, keep both hands above the table. Second, learn quickly to handle chopsticks so that you need not ask for Western-style implements. Do not be concerned if the cloth or table is splattered in a family meal, but care should be taken at a banquet to be neat. Napkins are used in many restaurants, but if they are not available, you may use the edge of the tablecloth. Damp towels or finger bowls with lemon will be used after dishes that are especially messy. Chewing and talking at the same time is considered appropriate behavior at the table, or even belching if need be, although some discretion is appropriate. Each table will be supplied with soy sauce, but there are unwritten laws as to its use: put soy sauce on dark-colored foods but salt with dishes that are light-colored, and never put soy sauce directly on your rice.

At family meals and in informal settings, you may raise your rice bowl to your mouth so that rice may be stroked into the mouth, but do not do so at a banquet. Noodles served in broth may be eaten by raising the noodles to one's mouth with the chopsticks, eating a portion of those noodles and lowering the remaining noodles back into the broth.

The most important rule of all is, as always, to observe your hosts and imitate their behavior. As in any culture, manners reflect background, and there are many different styles in Hong Kong. Don't be nervous, though, about making faux pas. The Chinese are extremely understanding of westerners, so enjoy yourself.

Entertaining at Home

If you entertain Chinese guests in your home, have plenty of fruit juices and soft drinks on hand. Avoid serving cheese and milk products since they are not a customary part of Chinese diet (although the success of Pizza Hut in Hong Kong belies their intolerance of cheese). In Chinese cuisine all vegetables, including lettuce, are cooked. Thus, your guests will feel awkward at being served salads, except for fruit salads. If you are serving meats, such as steaks or roasts, try to serve the meat in small chunks. Unless your guests have had extensive experience in the West, large pieces of meat that must be cut before being eaten will be problematic. Finally, avoid serving meats that are rare and bloody; they are repulsive to the Chinese.

OTHER ASPECTS OF CHINESE ETIQUETTE

Greetings

There is a long tradition of elaborate greetings in Chinese society. When you arrive at the airport, you will see groups of people, young and old, gathered to greet a returning family member or friend. Partly a family outing, partly a welcome home ceremony, these greeting parties begin at the customs gate and proceed to the airport restaurant for a welcoming beverage. Farewell parties proceed in reverse; that is, it begins with shared refreshment and then meanders to the departure gate, where a series of farewells is given to the departing guest, friend, or family member. It is customary to present small gifts to people as they are leaving Hong Kong. If you are receiving a gift, accept it graciously and open it later unless pressed by the group to open it immediately. Try to learn a few Cantonese or Mandarin greetings even before you arrive in Hong Kong. The use of English is more than appropriate, but the use of Chinese signals an additional graciousness and cultural warmth. A common form of greeting, as mentioned earlier, is *Neih sik faan mei ah?* (Have you eaten rice yet?), which really means "Hello and welcome." Small talk about generalities usually follows as an extension of the greeting. It is interesting in Chinese society that food is introduced as a form of greeting. Some believe that this custom comes from China's rural society, where people had to travel over many hours to meet. Therefore, it was polite and often necessary to inquire if your guest was hungry. For the Chinese, as well as other cultural groups, serving food is a sign of hospitality and a source of bonding. Similarly, when you receive visitors in your office or home, always invite them to be seated and offer them a beverage. Tea is the most common, but coffee, juice, or soda are also fine.

Leave-taking offers another opportunity to honor your guests. You will note that the Chinese walk their guests to the door and frequently see them to their cars, waiting in view while the car pulls away. Again, the root of this custom comes from older times, when a host or family would walk a ways on the path with the departing relative or friend.

Visiting Chinese Homes

As noted earlier, because of cramped living quarters, most Chinese do not entertain in their homes. Usually, only the upper class or upper-middle class Chinese have the space to do so. Also, there is a long tradition in Hong Kong of entertaining by eating out or by going to social clubs. If you *are* invited to a home, however, bring a small gift, usually a selection of fruit, which can be easily and quickly purchased at a local stand. The merchant will arrange an even number of apples or oranges and wrap them up as a gift package. Candy, spirits, or flowers are also acceptable gifts. Many expatriates bring candy and cookie products from their home countries for special gifts. If you bring spirits, do not expect that the wine or brandy will be served. Gifts are usually accepted and opened later after the guests have left.

When dining in a Chinese home, guests usually leave shortly after the end of the meal. You may wish to leave a small "packet" for the maid or cook if it is obvious that the meal was prepared especially for you, or, at the least, be sure to thank the household staff for their service and praise them in front of your host. If you should be a houseguest in the home of a Chinese family, leave some money for the *amah* (maid).

To Shove or Not to Shove

For all that is written about the courtesy of the Chinese people and the importance of deference and the emphasis on honorifics in the Confucian system, one would think that such courtesy might extend to public behavior as well. It doesn't. Expatriates are often puzzled, if not offended, by the disregard the crowds of Hong Kong demonstrate with their pushing and shoving. Attempting to board an out-island ferry on weekends or the MTR at rush hour defies the Confucian notion of courtesy—he clearly did not write for twentieth-century urban living. These extremes of behavior result from the Chinese distinction between inside and outside groups. Inside groups are composed of layers, the first of which is the family. As trust is established with others, a familylike relationship develops. In a fashion, people are adopted into a family and affectionately referred to as auntie and uncle and younger or older brother/sister. These make up the second layer. The third layer of affiliation includes classmates, fellow office workers, and members of neighborhood or ancestral associations. All others are considered outsiders, and, consequently, the rules of courtesy and accountability do not apply. As a result, behaviors that expatriates often experience as rude, such as cutting ahead in a line or pushing past people to meet a friend, are an accepted, if not valued, part of Chinese public behavior. For the insider, there is no responsibility to the outsider. As an old Chinese saying illustrates: "Sweep the snow in front of your own dwelling, but don't bother with the frost on the roof of others." Expatriates who come from cultures where politeness toward others in public is expected will have difficulty with the public discourteousness they regularly encounter. While it may injure the foreigner's sensitivity, the Chinese have no real consciousness of it being offensive.

Shopping and Bargaining

Hong Kong has long been known as a shopper's paradise where, through careful bargaining, the skillful shopper can do very well. There is a common notion in Hong Kong that there is a tourist price, a resident expatriate price, and a Chinese price. Today, most major stores operate on a fixed-price system. Nonetheless, bargaining remains a major part of ordinary business in Hong Kong and many other Asian countries; stores in the open markets and small bazaars, such as Stanley Market or the Kowloon Night Markets, still bargain. Besides the obvious purpose of setting a price, bargaining also establishes a relationship which measures the skills of the consumer against those of the merchant. A frequent mistake newcomers make during their efforts in the bargaining process is to attempt to extract too great a reduction in price as well as to try to bargain about small amounts of money. Both strategies indicate a lack of understanding of the basis of bargaining. There is a sense of justice that one should keep in mind that not only reflects the socioeconomic class of the merchants but that of the barterers as well. After living in Hong Kong for a time, you too may be embarrassed when you see an expatriate attempting to outdo the street hawkers over pennies.

Keep the following ideas in mind. First and foremost, bargaining is an interpersonal activity, so politeness is in order. Traders want to gain as much as they can since it is their livelihood; and they are never in a hurry, so they have an advantage. Take your time. Bargain, talk, bargain, talk again, continue to bargain. Suggest you will shop around, then wait and relax. Avoid displays of anger, but by all means express dubiousness or astonishment at the price. Always know in your own mind what you are willing to pay. If that merchant doesn't comply, remember there is always another who has the same merchandise and who will be willing to entertain your business. Sometimes the time of day is important. An antique dealer or jeweler may wish to sell you something early in the morning since it is a sign of good luck and will set the tone for sales during the day. Other merchants may have had a poor day, and a sale late in the day with a small margin of profit may be better than no sale at all.

Being an informed consumer is the best bargaining advice; check with other expatriates and Chinese colleagues for tips. A reasonable reduction is commonly thought to be anywhere from 10 to 40 percent. Also, consult with the Hong Kong Tourist Association. Their publications serve well as a guide to bargaining, receipts, guarantees, and other customs. Stores that are members of the association display its symbol in the window and provide reliable service.

ETIQUETTE COMMON THROUGHOUT ASIA

We will not attempt to provide a list of dos and don'ts for all of Asia. It would result in a gross oversimplification of the dynamics of cross-cultural interaction. However, there are some guidelines that can be helpful.

Gift-giving customs vary. In Japan, the giving of gifts is ritualistic and occurs in many circumstances; in other countries it is less pervasive. While small gifts related to hospitality or the making of business contacts (a small book, records, small items with a company logo, a bottle of cognac or brandy) are appropriate in most countries, more substantial gifts may be confused with bribes. Careful consultation with associates is necessary in evaluating the use of gift giving as an instrument in pursuing business objectives.

When traveling, be sure to ask the permission of anyone you wish to photograph. In some cultures adults are very sensitive to having their picture taken. If you do take pictures, try to share a copy with your subjects if possible.

Among Buddhists (particularly in Thailand, Burma, and parts of Japan) the head is generally considered to be the seat of the soul and is greatly respected. You will often see Asians bow their heads in respect when greeting or expressing farewells or when making an apology. While westerners may not be expected to act in this manner, a deferential nod will indicate respect.

If a Buddhist Asian is seated and you are standing, lean forward slightly to indicate respect, at least at the start of the conversation. This is a courteous gesture indicating that your head is not intentionally higher than his or hers, which would indicate that you believe you are either of higher rank or the dominant person in the encounter. Never pat a child on the head or stroke his or her face or hair. Also, try not to show the sole of your shoe, since the bottom of your foot is the lowest part of the body and displaying it insults those around you.

If you are entertaining Muslims (Malaysia, Indonesia, parts of China), remember that there are some major dietary restrictions. As you probably know, pork is considered unclean, but it is also important to be aware that Muslims consider dishes and cooking utensils which have touched pork to be contaminated (this includes lard or even cookies or crackers cooked with or containing pork fat). All use of alcohol is prohibited, including wine in the preparation of food. Dress codes for women in Muslim society are strict; women's shoulders and arms should be covered. When giving a gift, passing food, or giving and receiving money, the right hand only is used since the left hand is usually associated with unclean tasks. Shaking one's finger or beckoning with a crooked finger is rude.

Many words Western people have used in describing Asian society are actually quite ethnocentric. Words such as *Far East, Asiatic, native, backward, underdeveloped,* and *westernized* are not only skewed toward a European/North American view of history but frequently convey unfavorable connotations as well. Each of the countries of Asia has developed its own view of its culture, which may not be measured by the development of the European/North American economy. Listen carefully for the ethnocentric views we carry not only in the environment of work but also at Western social gatherings as we speak of Asian people.

7

Household Pointers

Establishing a new home is a big job, especially during the early months of your arrival, when a number of details must be tended to. The cost of living is high in Hong Kong, especially rent and car insurance. Thankfully, other costs are reasonable, such as food and household support staff. This chapter will provide information that will help you wade through the sea of details and tasks involved in settling into your new home and city. Hong Kong has a wealth of other resources as well to help you get settled: the Hong Kong Tourist Association, the Community Service Bureau, a large number of publications by the Hong Kong Government Press, and hundreds of civic and business clubs, hotels, and stores. Services such as Hong Kong Orientations provide expatriate relocation counselors to support you and your family during the transition.

HOUSING IN HONG KONG

Land is at a premium in Hong Kong, which contributes not only to overcrowding but also to escalating apartment prices and rents. Most expatriates live in flats (apartments in American English) in multistory apartment buildings or townhouses, no matter what their economic level or former life-style preferences are. As elsewhere, the size and location of the apartment are the variables which determine price. In the outlying areas of Hong Kong, in Sai Kung, the New Territories, and Lantau, one can find fairly reasonable townhouses and other rentals. However, they are at a considerable distance from most international schools. The Quarry Bay Tunnel, though, has greatly reduced the traveling time for residents in the Sai Kung/Clearwater Bay area, provided traffic is not congested. On the whole, North Americans usually avoid the outlying areas because of the traffic congestion and the long distance from the international schools. If, however, you do not have school-age children, consider Kowloon and the New Territories.

FINDING A SUITABLE HOME

The *South China Morning Post* has the most comprehensive listing of apartments to rent, share, or purchase. Most apartments will be managed by an agent who will assist you in viewing the property, and other apartments too if you wish. There are no multiple listings, so you may have to contact several agents to get the best overview of available housing. Some expatriates have been successful in approaching a building's management staff, who may be aware of apartments that are not listed or an apartment which will be available in the near future. Agents and some management groups receive one-half of the first month's rent as their fee. Be sure to clarify the fees before you enter into any agreement. Consult the Yellow Pages for a listing of realtors as well as relocation specialists, such as Hong Kong Orientations, a group of professionals who assist with expatriate relocation and cut the legwork of finding a flat in half.

Before you sign a contract, be sure you understand what is included in the rent plus any additional monthly fees. Try to have the government rates and management fees included in the rental price (rates are usually settled at 7.5 percent of the monthly rental fee). Depending on how interested you are in the property, you may wish to make these fees a point of negotiation. Utilities and additional parking and storage space are paid for separately. Also, attempt to structure your contract so you protect yourself from an exorbitantly high increase in rent during your rental period. Your landlord will require that you pay for the first month's rent along with an amount equal to two months' rent as a deposit, which is held as a guarantee against damages and from which the owner's portion of the agent commission will be deducted.

If at all possible, have your living arrangements settled, including a specific commitment of when your home will be available, before bringing your family to Hong Kong. This avoids a long stay in a hotel which not only can be costly for your company but also a drain on the family's psychic energy. Many hotels will provide fully serviced apartments.

LEAVE FLATS

An alternative to living in a hotel for weeks waiting for your apartment is to rent a leave flat. Many expatriates return home for two to four weeks in the summer and occasionally for longer periods at other times during the year. Through advertisements in a special section in the classifieds in the *South China Morning Post* or the bulletin boards at shopping centers, you may be able to find a suitable flat. It will come with all utilities and furniture and usually with the service of an amah. A security deposit of one month's rent is standard and the rent will include the cost of the amah.

If you choose to rent your flat during your own leave, be sure to secure all valuables and store any valued or treasured items. It is important to clarify with your landlord or your renter any particular rules that should be followed so that your agreement is clear.

HOUSEHOLD HELP

Many people hire amahs on a permanent basis. For those who have always managed their own homes, having permanent household staff is a new experience. Traditionally, there have been several types of support staff in Hong Kong: a wash amah, a cook amah, and a baby amah. Today such distinctions have disappeared, the amah's responsibilities combining all these functions. A good amah will usually do marketing, cooking, cleaning, laundry, and sometimes even driving. There are three major ethnic groups who generally hold these positions: Chinese, Thai, and Filipino.

The number of Chinese amahs who work in expatriate households is limited. Identified by their white and black uniforms, these women have clear ideas concerning the manner and extent of the work that they feel is appropriate for their position. Many young Chinese women believe there is more opportunity for work elsewhere in Hong Kong, so few enter this service. Thai and Philippine workers are sought by many expatriates since they are more accommodating to their employers' wishes. Due to the weak Philippine economy, many well-qualified and well-educated women work as amahs in Hong Kong, earning the major support for their families at home. Philippine amahs are known as hardworking, sometimes emotional in their responses, but extremely diligent and loyal. They are especially good with children.

The best way to secure an amah is to look in the *South China Morning Post* under "position wanted." Note especially the ads that are placed by people who are attempting to secure positions for their former employees. As many expatriates begin their repatriation process, they are anxious that their household staff find new positions, and, if their amahs were good employees, many do not wish to abandon them to families where they will be treated badly. Philippine amahs must return to their country two to four weeks after termination of their employment, so they also are anxious to get another appointment. If the ads in the paper do not produce sufficient results, go to the message boards at the local supermarkets. Frequently, the unemployed amah wants to stay in the same district where she has worked previously, and the local supermarket notice board provides an extremely effective way of circulating her name. Another avenue is to ask your closest neighbors if their amahs have a friend they would like to refer. Not surprisingly, many amahs like to have their friends working in the same community, if not the same building. Avoid placing an advertisement because you will receive more applicants than you can screen.

A note about references. Most former employees will give a letter of reference that identifies some of the qualities that were satisfactory, but they will probably not mention negative qualities. Therefore, it is important to read between the lines to determine what is not being said. If you have children, for example, it is important that the amah be mentioned in the letter as being good with children.

Inquire about current salaries when you arrive and try to start at the bottom of the scale with a promise of regular and rapid raises if things go well—then follow through with the raises. Make it clear that the first month is a trial period for both of you.

When hiring, remember that you interview the employee, not the reverse. It is not uncommon for someone to come with the person being interviewed and to even communicate for the person seeking employment. Don't confuse shyness with inadequate English competence. Shyness, which is common for newly arrived Philippine and Thai workers, can be dealt with, but a lack of English skills will create a serious household problem. Be sure, then, during the interview to ask the prospective employee enough questions directly to determine adequate English ability. Although the person will be living in your household, usually in a small room off the kitchen, remember that she is not being interviewed to join your family. A certain reserve and distance is appropriate and necessary for effective supervision of your staff. A mistake frequently made by people who have never had full-time household staff is to befriend their household employees. By maintaining an appropriate distance, you will gain more from your employee and avoid involvement in her personal life.

The health of your employee is of considerable importance to you since you will be responsible for paying doctor or hospital bills. Be sure to look at the date of their health certificates and check to see whether they have been inoculated for smallpox and diphtheria, that shots for typhoid and typhus are up-to-date, and that they do not have hepatitis. If you are not satisfied, and if the applicant does not have a doctor, arrange for an examination and inoculations. The Hong Kong Baptist Clinic, 222 Waterloo Road, Kowloon, provides a clinic which will be helpful in this matter. Since most employers pay medical expenses for their household help, insurance is important. There are two kinds of insurance: workers' compensation and personal comprehensive liability policy. By law you are required to have employee compensation insurance to cover any injury sustained by your employee while working for you. Consult an agent to determine if a comprehensive personal liability policy would add additional coverage and would be appropriate for your particular needs. Employers are also responsible for providing live-in maids with work clothes.

Be aware that the employer is required to send the worker back home every two years for a one- to two-week vacation period. During that time, a small daily stipend is expected. If you have a Chinese amah, you are expected to give an additional month's salary for the Chinese New Year.

Consult the Hong Kong Immigration Department guidelines for hiring Filipina, Thai, and Sri Lankan amahs. These guidelines will outline the structure of the contract as well as your obligations. Many expatriates initially use an employment agency that guides them through the process as well as assists in verifying the employee's work experience and helps guarantee both the employer and employee's rights. Again, word of mouth and the experience of other expatriates will alert you to the better agencies.

PEST CONTROL

If you have never lived in a semitropical locale, a delightful discovery awaits you—the gecko, a small lizardlike creature that chooses to live with humans. The gecko is a friend whose role in life is to eat the insects it can capture within your home. They are harmless, entertaining little critters who will create excitement as they dash out of the most unexpected places.

Another less pleasant surprise is the flying cockroach and also the ordinary crawling variety that are ever present in the summer. Their presence is not related to any lapse in standards of cleanliness but rather to the tropical nature of Hong Kong. A wide variety of aerosol repellents is available as well as the services of many pest control companies.

People who live on ground level in less congested areas, such as the outlying islands or even the wooded areas of the Peak, may find an occasional visiting snake. Ask the police to remove it since there are still some poisonous snakes in Hong Kong, including the Chinese cobra, the pit viper or bamboo snake, the coral snake, and the krait.

SHOPPING

Whether Hong Kong's reputation as a shopper's paradise is still deserved is questionable. However, by taking some care and getting a good briefing as to what the preferred stores are, the expatriate can be quite a successful shopper. But remember the old motto, "caveat emptor" (buyer beware!). Take special care regarding any purchase that is expensive, especially jewelry, including jades and gold; antiques, which should have a certificate; and watches or any other product, such as designer bags, which are frequently contraband or counterfeit.

When selecting shops, begin with those that have been personally recommended. Other reliable sources of information are the lists produced by the various chambers of commerce, the Hong Kong Tourist Association, and the Community Advice Bureau.

Some shops have established reputations for fair service to expatriates. But there are also plenty of crooks. Avoid the touts who promise to lead you to a "special" friend. Usually these people prey on the uninformed tourist. While the resulting experience may be an interesting cultural adventure, you will pay more for the item and its quality will be doubtful.

Clothing

For nonluxury items, such as everyday clothes, ask local people for recommendations. As was said earlier, there is no bargaining in department stores, and shopping is simple. Sometimes discounts are available, but the policy varies from store to store; be sure to ask "what is your best price?"—it never hurts. You can get sturdy clothing of every kind—shirts, pajamas, underwear, etc.—but quality will vary. Westerners often buy sweaters, pants, jackets, and stockings in street stalls and the alleys as well as in major stores. Li Yuen Street (East and West) in Central, Granville Road in Tsim Sha Tsui, Stanley Village Market, Poor Man's Nightclub, in front of the Macau Ferry Terminal at night, and Kowloon Evening Market at Temple Street sell shirts, T-shirts, sweaters, blue jeans, etc., originally made for export to the United States and Europe. Sizes are usually Western, and the prices are attractive for these seconds and overruns. Specialized street markets are also worth visiting, such as the Jade Market on Kansu Street in Tsim Sha Tsui; Cloth Alley on Wing On Street; and the bird market near the Mongkok MTR Station. There are also a number of factory outlet stores. For the specific addresses, buy one of the current books about shopping in Hong Kong. Several books worth mentioning are Barbara Anderson-Tsang's *Hong Kong Shopping Guide,* Dana Goetz's *Hong Kong Factory Bargains* and *Hong Kong—Yin and Yang,* and the Hong Kong Tourist Association's monthly *Official Guidebook.*

World-famous tailors make suits and shirts at less than Western prices, and by living in Hong Kong you will have the time to work with your tailor for the best fit and style. Remember that misunderstandings about your detailed specifications for your order can occur because of language problems or differences in taste. Have an adequate number of fittings and watch the progress of the work carefully until you and your tailor really know each other. It is difficult to find large, Western-size shoes in Hong Kong, but they can be made to order.

Guarantees and Receipts

Keep all your receipts. They may be required for import or insurance requirements upon repatriation. If you have any complaints about your purchase, present your receipt to the Consumer Council and request action on your behalf. Usually, local guarantees on goods are valid for one year. Check the guarantee on all photographic, electronic, and electrical equipment as well as watches for their world-wide/international guarantee. Local retailers will not carry any guarantees. Be sure all receipts and guarantees carry a full description of the goods purchased as well as the seal of the store.

Marketing and Food

Milk is safe when bought from licensed dairies such as Dairy Farm, a conglomerate that owns a dairy and a chain of supermarkets. The Chinese do not generally like butter and cheese but you can, of course, buy them in the markets.

Most people send their house staff each day to buy their produce, meats, and fish in the local market. Local beef is not generally purchased by the European community, who prefer to buy beef imported from New Zealand. Local meat and poultry are excellent for Chinese and Asian cuisine. Canned foods are imported and expensive. Frozen foods are available, but most people rely on fresh produce.

Drinking water is heavily chlorinated and is treated according to international standards. While it is not always necessary to boil it for drinking purposes, many residents do so as an added precaution. Some districts of Hong Kong are old and their water pipelines may be rusty. It is easy to buy bottled water, and some expatriates prefer it to the taste of chlorinated tap water. In general, avoid nonbottled water when traveling in Hong Kong and Asia.

Many international brands of soft drinks are available in Hong Kong as is a wide selection of alcoholic drinks. Wines come from Europe, the United States, and Australia, and the better food stores in Central and Kowloon are well stocked. The Chinese prefer brandy, rice wine, and beer. Avoid ordering mixed drinks in Chinese restaurants since they have neither the experience in preparing them nor the ingredients to make them properly.

There are a variety of services to facilitate household shopping in Hong Kong. You can arrange with your local grocer or some supermarkets to have your delivery sent daily to your home and your bills rendered monthly or placed on a bank payment card. Fresh food is cheaper at the outdoor markets although prices fluctuate greatly depending on the condition of the product. Prices are listed daily in the newspapers. Your cook will almost surely be able to get better prices than you can, so you may want to leave the shopping to her or him.

There are many supermarkets available, but in areas of the city where the expatriate community dominates, local markets are used to accommodate its needs and carry American and European products. Occasionally, items will not be available. While there is no need to hoard, you will want to plan ahead, especially for ingredients wanted for special family or holiday celebrations. The major westernized chains in Hong Kong are Park 'n Shop and Wellcome. USA and Colorado Company and Olivers provide specialized products that are difficult to secure as well as a variety of gourmet items.

Weights and Measures

Hong Kong follows the metric system, and you will probably want to carry a conversion table when you shop until you have learned to think metrically. In addition, Hong Kong also uses the Chinese system to purchase meat, fish, and vegetables in the market. A *catty* is equal to 1.3 pounds. A *picul* is used by wholesalers and is equal to 22.7 pounds. The *chek* is approximately equal to our foot, but it may vary from 11 ½ inches to 14 ½ inches, depending on which trade is using it. Each ch'ek is divided into ten *ts'im,* and each ts'im into ten *fan.*

SECURITY

Hong Kong is a reasonably safe community, but, as in all major cities, care should be taken. If you need assistance, contact the local police station. Policemen who speak English wear a red flash, or ribbon, under their shoulder badge. There is a long tradition of using iron gates on doors and windows. Major apartment complexes have a security gate with a watchman as well as intercoms and television systems to screen prospective visitors. Be sure to secure your doors at all times. All iron safety doors and windows have locks. Your front doors will be double-keyed and dead-bolted. Your windows may have iron grills that are locked.

8

Schools

THE HONG KONG EDUCATIONAL SYSTEM

Hong Kong is rather exceptional in its educational offerings, which reflect the international nature of a city where not only Chinese, Americans, and British but also Germans, Swiss, French, Canadians, Koreans, Japanese, and Norwegians live in substantial numbers. Each national community provides its own educational services.

The Hong Kong Department of Education offers free primary education from grades 1 through 6 and junior secondary education from grades 7 through 9, or as they are referred to, forms 1 through 3. Senior secondary education continues through forms 4 and 5, which fulfills the five-year educational sequence leading to the Hong Kong Certificate of Education. After completing the HKCE testing successfully, a student may continue academic studies for two years (forms 6 and 7) and then take the Hong Kong Advanced Level Examination (HKALE, or "A" level). On completion of one's A levels, a student is prepared for one of the regional postsecondary opportunities or undergraduate work abroad. Cantonese is used in most of the courses associated with the Hong Kong Department of Education schools, although there is a commitment to increase the competencies in English and Putunghua. Although the Hong Kong government has guaranteed nine years of education to all of its children through the public schools, the child whose primary language is English must rely on the private school system, which offers excellent opportunities at all levels.

Most expatriates do not place their children in Chinese schools, since the educational gain of learning to read Chinese and speak Cantonese, if even attainable, does not outweigh the potential academic loss. Unlike many European languages which can be learned in a relatively short time, Chinese is too difficult to simultaneously learn and use as the medium for instruction. The best option for a broader Chinese educational environment but with course work in English is the Chinese International School. Most expatriates, however, choose to place their children in either the American or British private school systems of Hong Kong.

American and British educational systems are strikingly different from each other. Under the British system, elementary school children enter first grade by age five, rather than age six, and are placed solely by age. If your child was advanced a year, he or she could be held back. The British schools do not encourage close ties between home and school; parental participation in their children's course work is uncommon.

At the secondary level, the differences become profound. In the American system a student will study a subject in depth for one or two semesters. European schools are designed so that the student studies many courses in the same subject at one time. The topic is divided into units, which are taught throughout the years of secondary education. Thus, a student studying math in a European setting will be working on units of algebra, geometry, and trigonometry simultaneously while the American student takes the courses consecutively, with a semester or a year spent on each. Because of these different curriculum structures, transfers from the European to the American system after the age of thirteen are quite difficult since the American student will not have the necessary proficiency in his or her courses to return to an advanced level in the United States schools.

Grade levels are also structured differently. In British schools as well as the Hong Kong Board of Education schools, the students complete grades 1 to 6 in primary school. At the beginning of the U.S. seventh grade, however, British and Hong Kong students enter form 1 and continue at least to form 5. After completing form 5, students usually sit for the General Certificate of Education, or GCE exams.

Starting at age thirteen, students will take the same subjects for two to three years until they feel ready to take the GCE exam in any five subjects. During this period, there are no grades given or credits earned toward graduation. In fact, there is no graduation process as there is in the United States, where a person is given a diploma. Students planning to attend a university complete forms 6 and 7 studying three subjects in depth to prepare for the advanced level exams. To qualify for university admission, students must pass five GCE exams and three A-level exams. Because leaving secondary school is based on passing the GCEs and not on grade level completed, the British system is open-ended. Each exam is given only once a year, and students can sit for exams as many times as they wish.

ENGLISH LANGUAGE SCHOOLS

When you select a school, consider your child's overall educational needs and identify the specific instructional system into which the child will be placed upon repatriation or during a future posting. Some Americans choose the British or German/Swiss schools at the primary level to diversify their child's education and increase language and cross-cultural skills during the formative primary years. By and large most expatriates choose an educational system for secondary schools that enables their adolescent children to fit back into their national system easily. Thus, most Americans choose the American educational system in Hong Kong for ease of transition into stateside high schools or American universities and colleges.

If possible, choose a school system prior to your departure. You can contact the Hong Kong Tourist Information Office in the city nearest you, the British Consul, or the school itself to begin the application process. Most of the schools are crowded, so you will want to apply as far in advance as possible.

There are three major classifications of schools in Hong Kong:

schools that follow the American school system, schools associated with the English Schools Foundation and the British system, and the private school system, which addresses the interests of special national groups.

American System

Hong Kong International School (HKIS) (6-23 South Bay Close, Repulse Bay, Hong Kong; tel: 8122305; fax: 8127037; cable: HKISCHOOL) established in 1966; approximately 1,800 students with a capacity for 2,100; nursery school through grade 12.

This coeducational day school is governed by an appointed board of managers for the Lutheran Church-Missouri Synod and is accredited by the Western Association of Schools and Colleges. Its two major campuses are located in residential areas on the south side of Hong Kong Island. The new high school building is located at Red Hill Road, Tai Tam, some five miles from the elementary and middle school campus in Repulse Bay. The two campuses, occupying ten acres, consist of classroom buildings, an auditorium, three libraries, two cafeterias, a staffed infirmary, a covered play area, tennis courts, three gymnasiums, playing fields, two squash courts, three science labs, computer labs, two swimming pools, a language lab, an art room, and a chapel-auditorium. A full program of sports and extracurricular activities is available as well as special programs for advanced placement and independent study. French, Spanish, Cantonese, and Mandarin are taught. The school maintains a teacher/student ratio of 1/12. The elementary school uses individual and team approaches to education. A provisional kindergarten and primary facility has recently been established on Kennedy Road. The high school focuses on college preparation. Ninety-eight percent of the graduates have attended colleges such as Cornell, Brown, Northwestern, Rice, and Stanford. PSAT, SAT, ACT, and TOEFL are given as well as the Iowa Test of Basic Skills and National Educational Development. Approximately 60 percent of the students are citizens of the United States and 30 percent are of Asian heritage, a large number of these being Asian-Americans as well as children from Japan, Korea, and Taiwan. No uniforms are required in the high school.

Applicants for admission must speak English, must have had a physical examination within the past six months, and must present their current school record prior to acceptance. Children must be five years of age by October 31 to enter grade one. If you or your company purchases a debenture or bond, currently HK$70,000 or approximately US$10,000, your child will be guaranteed admission if he or she meets the other admissions requirements. Students from the United States and other international schools have priority. The school year runs from August to June.

HKIS offers a full counseling program that supports its students and their families during the initial adjustment to Hong Kong as well as throughout the child's enrollment in the school. Both peer and professional counseling are available. Children with moderate special education needs can be accommodated, but the wide range of special services accessible in the United States is generally not available.

English Schools Foundation

English Schools Foundation (ESF) (42B Stubbs Road, Hong Kong; tel: 5742351; fax: 8380957) established in 1969; approximately 3,000 students in four secondary schools through form 7; 4,000 students in nine primary schools; nursery schools.

These coeducational, nonprofit day schools provide educational services to children who, because of language or national origin, either cannot or choose not to attend the government-sponsored Chinese-speaking schools. Although over forty nationalities are represented in the schools, 50 percent of the students are from the United Kingdom and another 25 percent are from English-speaking countries. The Hong Kong government subsidizes the basic educational costs of these schools on an equal basis with the Chinese schools. Tuition includes the cost of hiring foreign nationals as teachers and other special services directed at the needs of expatriate children. Students with special educational needs and learning disabilities are serviced through the school's Special Education Center as well as through services in two secondary schools and two primary schools. The ESF-sponsored school curriculum is set by the Department of Education and Science in London. The schools are accredited by the London University Schools Examination Board. Applications for entrance may be secured at the school nearest your home. If a place is not available in a school in your catchment area, your child will be assigned to another location. PSAT, SAT, ACT, A-level, A/S-level, GCSE, Pitman, and RSA tests are given. The teacher/student ratio is approximately 1/16. Students must wear uniforms. The Foundation schools include the following:

Primary Schools

Beacon Hill School, 23 Ede Road, Kowloon Tong; tel: 3365221.

Boundary Junior School, 4 Rose Street, Yau Yat Tsuen; tel: 3814362.

Bradbury Junior School, 43C Stubbs Road, Hong Kong; tel: 5748240.

Glenealy Junior School, Horney Road, Hong Kong; tel: 5221919.

Kennedy Road Junior School, 19 Sha Wan Drive, Sandy Bay Pokfulam; tel: 8550711.

Kowloon Junior School, 20 Perth Street, Kowloon; tel: 7145279.

Peak School, 20 Plunkett's Road, Hong Kong; tel: 8497211.

Quarry Bay Junior School, 6 Hau Yuen Path, Braemar Hill, North Point; tel: 5664242.

Shatin Junior School, 3 Lai Wo Lane, Fotan, Shatin NT; tel: 6922721.

Secondary Schools

Island School, 20 Borrett Road, Hong Kong; tel: 5247135.

King George V School, 2 Tin Kwong Road, Kowloon; tel: 7113028.

Shatin College, Lai Wo Lan, Fotan, Shatin NT; tel: 6991811.

South Island School, 50 Nam Fung Road, Aberdeen; tel: 5559313.

Special Education

Special education for the expatriate child is limited. Parents who are accustomed to a wide range of special education services addressing learning disabilities and behavior disorders will not experience the breadth of services that they have become accustomed to receiving at home. The Hong Kong International School, as noted previously, provides some services for moderately learning-disabled children. The English School Foundation staffs the Sarah Roe Center (2A Tin Kwong Road, Homantin, Kowloon; tel: 7600441). This center is designed to address the needs of severely handicapped and learning-disabled students. Contact the center well in advance of any relocation to assess its ability to address the specific requirements of your child.

Private National Schools System

Most national schools focus on the specialized needs of their citizens with the hope that the expatriate child will be well prepared to make a smooth transition back into the national school system upon repatriation. Children from the countries involved are usually guaranteed a place in these national schools.

California International U.S.A. School (143 Waterloo Road, Kowloon Tong; tel: 3051077) approximately 240 students; grades 1 through 12.

Established in 1986, this school follows the American system, providing educational services mostly to the English-speaking Chinese (60 percent) and other Asian nationals (40 percent). The teacher/student ratio is approximately 1/20.

Chinese International School (CIS) (10 Borrett Road, Hong Kong; tel: 5244181; fax 8401659) established in 1982; approximately 750 students; nursery to form 5.

This bilingual (Mandarin, English), bicultural, coeducational day school follows the British and Hong Kong systems and is governed by the Chinese International School Foundation. The GCE is given at the completion of form five. The teacher/student ratio is 1/14. Uniforms are required.

German Swiss International School (GSIS) (11 Guilford Road, The Peak, Hong Kong; tel: 8496216) established in 1969; approximately 1,000 students; nursery school through form 6.

Considered by many to be the best of the private international schools, GSIS maintains a German curricular stream (approximately 400 students) and an English stream (approximately 600 students). There is a two-year waiting list for the English stream, which follows the curriculum of the Department of Education and Science in London. The teacher/student ratio is 1/25. Uniforms are required.

Hong Kong Japanese School (157 Blue Pool Road, Hong Kong; tel: 5745479) established in 1966; approximately 1,700 children; primary one to form 3.

Korean International School (85 Smithfield Street, Kennedy Town; tel: 8551430) established in 1927; approximately 120 students; grades six to twelve.

L'Ecole Française International (French International School) (30 Price Road, Jardine's Lookout, Hong Kong; tel: 5776217) approximately 800 students; kindergarten through form 7.

Enrollment in this school is restricted to debenture holders. The English stream begins with nursery school and continues through form 5. The French stream accepts children for Petite Maternelle at age three through the Baccalaureate.

Norwegian School in Hong Kong (5 Cox's Path, Kowloon; tel: 3674438) established in 1989; approximately 50 students; Norwegian syllabus.

Royden House School (110-18 Caine Road, Hong Kong; tel: 5475479) established in 1939; approximately 500 students; kindergarten to form 7; English syllabus.

SEA Canadian Overseas Secondary School (166-166A Boundary Street, Kowloon; tel: 3611167) established in 1983; approximately 450 students.

ENROLLMENT IN HONG KONG UNIVERSITIES AND POLYTECHNICS

Admission to Hong Kong universities and postsecondary institutions such as the polytechnics is very competitive. For that reason expatriates are rarely accepted as internal, or regular degree, students. Exceptions have been made, usually for mature students as well as for people who have a longer-lasting relationship with Hong Kong. Expatriates can, however, enroll as external students at Hong Kong University as well as at Chinese University. Contact the registrar at the following addresses for current information:

Hong Kong University, Pokfulam Road, Hong Kong
Chinese University of Hong Kong, Shatin, New Territories
University of Science and Technology (UST), Clearwater Bay, Hong Kong
University of East Asia, Taipei Island, Macao
Hong Kong Polytechnic, Hunghom, Kowloon
City Polytechnic of Hong Kong, Argyle Center, Tower 2, 700 Nathan Road, Kowloon

United States-Affiliated Colleges

Hong Kong Baptist College (224 Waterloo Road, Kowloon; tel: 3397333) is affiliated with Ohio University in Athens, Ohio, and one may continue or supplement one's education. Credits earned at HKBC are transferable to some American universities. Consult the registrar at your home college or university to determine if they will accept credits from HKBC. The Council on International Educational Exchange (CIEE) (205 E. 42nd Street, New York, NY 10017; tel: (212) 661-1414) is an excellent resource for identifying alternative strategies for studying in Hong Kong and Asia. The University of Michigan is a good example of such opportunities. On a yearly basis, members of its education department send staff to Hong Kong to lecture in an independent study program in education.

Extramural Studies

Excellent extramural courses at the universities provide opportunities for continuing education. The University of Hong Kong offers courses at the main campus or at the Extramural Studies Town Centre in Central. The Department of Extramural Studies of Chinese University offers many courses at its Shatin campus. Many expatriates study Chinese language and culture, although there is also a wide range of courses offered in English.

NURSERY SCHOOLS

There is a variety of preschools in Kowloon and Hong Kong which accept four- and five-year-old English-speaking children. Some also accept three-year-olds. An official list of the schools may be obtained from the Community Advice Bureau. According to Hong Kong law, anyone can start a nursery provided that the numbers are kept small. These home groups provide a valuable service. In addition to the Community Advice Bureau, you may want to ask your neighbors and colleagues about the reputations of these groups and get their recommendations.

There are also a number of professional nurseries which serve English-speaking children. Their approach and methods vary, so you may want to consult the Hong Kong Pre-School Playgroups Association (GDO Box 4049, Hong Kong) for more detailed information concerning each group.

9

Health and Medical Care

HEALTH CONDITIONS IN HONG KONG

Hong Kong, even though it is tropical, is a relatively comfortable city and is free of major tropical diseases. People in good health have little difficulty. Because of an extremely humid climate, however, sufferers from sinus problems, hay fever, asthma, and other respiratory problems may experience discomfort. Pink eye, some fungus troubles, and ear infections are also common; many believe these are due to the high bacteria count in the water at the public beaches. Sewage control is not as effective as in other international cities and care should be taken during the summer months. Athlete's foot is a frequent complaint (known as "Hong Kong foot").

Hong Kong health officials report the lowest rate of tuberculosis in the area; nevertheless, annual X rays are recommended for babies and young adults. As mentioned earlier, routine immunizations—polio, diphtheria and tetanus—are advised but not required. If you plan to travel in other Asian countries, however, you may need more extensive immunizations (check with your doctor). In addition to going to your regular physician, you can be inoculated at the Port Health Inoculation Centers. One is in Wanchai and the other in Tsim Sha Tsui.

Public health management and sanitation services are good. Meats and fish sold in the markets and served in public eating places are strictly inspected and controlled. Some freshwater fish raised in the fish farms of the New Territories may, however, have intestinal parasites, so always cook fish and seafood well. All vegetables should be thoroughly washed since produce in Hong Kong comes from Guangzhou Province, where farmers rely on night soil (human waste) as a fertilizer. Plumbing and sewage systems are adequate in all modern buildings but leave something to be desired in older buildings and hillside areas. Any coloring or sediment found in the water usually comes from antiquated water pipes. To be on the safe side, many people, as noted earlier, choose to boil and/or filter their water or use bottled water (the water is fluorinated). Streets are cleaned and monitored regularly. Municipal pest control does its best with extermination, but mosquitos can be bothersome, especially during the summer months. If you do not live in an air-conditioned unit, use a mosquito net and/or rely on mosquito coils. Periodically, rabies have surfaced; therefore, officials are strict about inoculation of all domestic animals.

In Hong Kong there are very few quarantinable diseases, with fewer than 100 cases of malaria reported each year. Viral hepatitis A, however, is endemic and gamma globulin injections at four- to six-month intervals are frequently advised. Hepatitis B accounts for 25 percent of all reported hepatitis cases in Hong Kong and is widespread in Southeast Asia. People who are in close contact with local populations, body fluids, blood products (blood transfusions), acupuncture instruments, tattoo needles, ear-piercing equipment, and dental and medical tools should be inoculated.

There have been relatively few cases (thirteen in 1991) of AIDS reported in Hong Kong since its first appearance in 1985. There are currently procedures for screening the blood for HRV antibodies. If you are traveling, you may wish to consult your national office of the World Health Organization for current information on the areas you will visit. Blood for transfusions has been screened in Hong Kong since 1985. In the unlikely event that you need a blood transfusion, it is prudent to inquire about the screening practices used. The use of plasma expanders rather than blood transfusions should also be considered. To inquire about the quality of blood and proper medical equipment if transfusion is needed, contact the local Red Cross in Hong Kong or write to the Institute of Virus Research, Kyoto University, Sakyoku, Kyoto 606, Japan.

As said before, be sure that your tetanus and polio shots are updated. For those born since 1956 who have not had measles or the measles vaccination, a vaccination is advisable. You may wish to contact the U.S. Government Printing Office, which publishes a booklet entitled "Health Information for International Travel" (see chapter 12 for more information). The Center for Disease Control in Maryland offers a twenty-four-hour hot line for international travelers (404-332-4559), which provides the most current information on immunization requirements and information on any recent disease outbreaks in Hong Kong or other parts of Asia.

FINDING RELIABLE HEALTH CARE

Hospitals

Hong Kong has many hospitals; major specialty clinics, known as polyclinics, providing specific medical care such as pediatric, gynecological, dental, and most major services; public out-patient clinics; and floating clinics and "flying doctors" that service the more isolated island communities. The largest hospitals under the direction of the government have a twenty-four-hour casualty department: Princess Margaret Hospital in Lai Chi Kok, Queen Elizabeth Hospital in Kowloon, Queen Mary Hospital in Pokfulam, Tang Shiu Kin Hospital in Western, and Prince of Wales Hospital in Shatin. Several private or subsidized hospitals frequently used by expatriates are St. Theresa's Hospital in Kowloon Tong and Baptist Hospital with outpatient clinics in Kowloon; Hong Kong Adventist Hospital (twenty-four-hour emergency dental and medical services and specialty clinics with an expatriate staff and an outpatient department Sunday through Friday noon) in the Mid-Levels; Canossa Hospital located above Central; and the Matilda and War Memorial Hospital situated on the Peak. Most hospitals either have a resident doctor or one on call at all times. Shortly after arriving in Hong Kong, take the time to visit one or two of the hospitals to become familiar with them. While expatriates have used all the major hospital services in Hong Kong, most English-speaking expatriates have found the Hong Kong Adventist Hospital, Matilda Hospital, and Canossa Hospital most accommodating. Visit and talk to the staff to familiarize yourself with the services in the hospitals and also the manner for accessing them. Maternity care, pre- and postnatal classes, natural birth, and traditional delivery are available in Hong Kong. Consult the Yellow Pages of the telephone book for addresses and telephone numbers or call the Community Advice hot line.

Emergencies

Emergency ambulance services are available in Hong Kong and will take you to the nearest hospital in case of severe illness. The number for an ambulance and for police assistance is the same: 999.

Doctors, Dentists, and Medical Professionals

Medical services in Hong Kong are world class. The best resource, in Hong Kong or at home, for current names of doctors, dentists, dental hygienists, hospitals, and all other forms of medical care is friends, acquaintances, and colleagues who have used these services and can make recommendations. Because the number of professionals who have established expatriate clientele is small, their services are painstakingly scrutinized. Reputations are easily built and destroyed. Be sure to cross-reference referrals to be fully satisfied with your selection since, fair or not, stories are easily passed—and distorted—throughout the small expatriate community. Most medical professionals have received all or major parts of their training in the United Kingdom, North America, Australia, New Zealand, or Japan. Hong Kong also has its own school of dentistry and several medical schools. All registered medical practitioners are listed in the *Government Gazette* twice a year, and doctors are also, of course, listed in the Yellow Pages. Fee scales generally follow international standards. Expatriates from cultures where doctors provide time for patient-doctor dialogue concerning the medical implications of their treatment and who are accustomed to questioning their doctor's treatment or judgment may have difficulty with the distant and occasionally impersonal style of medical practitioners in Hong Kong.

Counseling Services

English-speaking expatriates seeking individual or family counseling and related support services will find a number of programs: Alcoholics Anonymous, Al-Anon, Al-Ateen, and Overeaters Anonymous. The Society for the Aid and Rehabilitation of Drug Abusers offers a hot line and referrals to English-speaking expatriates. The Marriage and Personal Counseling Service (MPCS) has a multinational staff well suited to address most emotional needs of expatriates. The Hong Kong Catholic Marriage Advisory Council, the Hong Kong Christian Service, the Yang Memorial Social Service Center, and the Christian Counseling Services associated with St. John's Cathedral can also be of help. The Hong Kong Samaritans provide an emergency hot line and referral service for those who may be experiencing extreme distress or suicidal feelings. The Hong Kong Adventist Hospital has specialized educational programs addressing such issues as smoking, weight management, and stress reduction. The Matilda Hospital provides a broad range of psychiatric and hospitalization services. There is a cancer hot line to assist patients and their families with adjustment issues. Consult your Yellow Pages or call the Social Service Department for current telephone numbers. If you prefer a private counselor, there is a variety of professionals from English-speaking countries who offer individual, group, and family counseling. Again, the informal expatriate referral network will provide you with recommendations.

Acupuncturists

Many expatriates have used acupuncture for eating disorders, smoking problems, stress, and pain reduction. The major difficulty with traditional Chinese medical arts is not the service but the language barrier: the practitioners are frequently monolingual. Be sure to verify the sterilization procedures of the needles used in acupuncture to avoid any contact with a contagious disease such as AIDS or hepatitis, which are transmitted through the inadvertent sharing of body fluids. Check the Yellow Pages or the expatriate resource books for current addresses.

PHARMACIES

Large, Western-style pharmacies (or, as they are known in Hong Kong, chemists or dispensaries) can be found in the major shopping malls and regional shopping centers throughout Hong Kong. Look for the names "Mannings" and "Watson's" since these large chains provide the best selection, quality, and quantity of products similar to the large national drugstores found in the United States and the United Kingdom. The pharmacies will accept only prescriptions written in Hong Kong. Doctors frequently fill their own prescriptions in their offices. Most drugs available elsewhere can also be found in Hong Kong, although perhaps not from the same pharmaceutical company as you are used to. After researching the availability of the medication, your local doctor will subscribe a generic name or trade name for a similar product if necessary. If you are worried about the availability of a special medication, you may simply want to bring a sufficient supply with you. If you have a medical condition requiring a fairly common drug, have your Hong Kong doctor write a current prescription.

If you are prescribed medicines by Asian doctors, be sure to ask the physician or pharmacist to check the correlation between dosage and body weight since dosages are frequently prescribed according to the scale of Asian bodies, which are generally smaller than Western. Many of the familiar remedies for headaches, colds, aches and pains, coughs, and constipation are available in the large dispensing pharmacies and the many local drugstores in Hong Kong, but you cannot always be sure of finding the product that you use. A plus side to this situation is that you may find products from a variety of global suppliers that will do the job and be quite effective.

Some expatriates have used Chinese medicines for particular ailments, but caution should be taken. Care should also be taken in purchasing drugs from the many small drugstores since Hong Kong entrepreneurs have been known to copy medications, sometimes not so accurately, and to sell products past their expiration dates. Both the Hong Kong Adventist Hospital and Queen Mary Hospital provide twenty-four-hour pharmaceutical services in the event of an emergency.

WORLDWIDE MEDICAL NETWORKS

Most expatriates feel comfortable in dealing with a medical emergency in their home surroundings and, after a while, also in Hong Kong. However, when you travel and find yourself in foreign cities without a network of friends and neighbors to help you and also without the language skills to interview the appropriate medical personnel, medical emergencies take on understandably frightening proportions. There are, thankfully, several groups that will help in identifying medical services in worldwide locations and thus alleviate at least some of your fear. You may wish to join one of the following.

International Association for Medical Assistance to Travelers (IAMAT)

IAMAT has developed a network of centers throughout most of the world. By writing to the U.S. or Canadian address given below, you can get a membership packet which includes a directory of IAMAT centers with addresses and phone numbers, an immunization chart, a personal medical record folder, and a membership card. This packet is sent free of charge, but IAMAT is largely supported by donations, and you will want to send a donation with your request. Thus, when you are traveling and need a doctor or emergency help, you will have a number to call for a list of approved doctors, both general practitioners and specialists, who are on duty for that particular twenty-four-hour period, including Sundays and holidays. These physicians are selected according to a review of their professional qualifications, their ability to speak English, and their acceptance of a fixed-fee schedule. You should allow at least six weeks for a response from IAMAT when you request the membership packet.

IAMAT has a center in Hong Kong at the Sing Tao Medical Center in Central. In the United States the IAMAT office is at 417 Center Street, Lewiston, NY 14092 (716-754-4883) and in Canada at 188 Nicklin Road, Guelph, ON N1H7L5 (519-836-0102).

Intermedic

Membership in this service can be obtained for a minimal fee. Members receive a directory of doctors in two hundred cities around the world, listing names, addresses, and office and home phone numbers. These doctors have agreed to a standard fee schedule and are well qualified. If no doctor is listed for your travel destination, you can call the nearest listed Intermedic doctor and ask for a referral.

When you apply, you will receive a membership card to show to physicians. Intermedic's main office is located at 777 Third Avenue, New York, NY 10017.

International SOS Assistance

International SOS Assistance will provide medical services to corporate employees, individual travelers, and expatriates, including the monitoring of an illness, referrals to English-speaking doctors and facilities in the area, and, if necessary, medical evacuation to the nearest treatment center or one's home country. Their services can be purchased on a weekly or yearly basis. For information, write to International SOS Assistance, P.O. Box 11568, Philadelphia, PA 19116 or call 1-800-523-8930.

Health Insurance

Citizens of the United Kingdom and nationals of the European Community are entitled to free or reduced-cost emergency medical care in Hong Kong. The medical and hospital insurance needs of citizens of the United States are usually met through the employers' medical packages. Blue Cross/Blue Shield is available in Hong Kong.

Consult your employer and policy for your restrictions and the method of reimbursement.

Services for the Disabled

The Rehabilitation Division of the Hong Kong Council of Social Services publishes a guide for physically disabled visitors and residents in Hong Kong which describes the accessibility of all major buildings in Hong Kong. Land transportation can be arranged through a special transportation service by calling "Dial-A-Ride" at 8178154. It is wise to make reservations well in advance.

10

Cars and Driving

AUTOMOBILES

The automobile is a luxury for some and for others a necessity. About 90 percent of Hong Kong's population depends on public transportation; approximately 150,000 private cars serve the remaining 10 percent. There has been and will be a continued effort on the part of the government to create deterrents to the purchase and use of private vehicles by increasing the first registration tax, the license fees, and the fuel tax. These measures have, in recent years, successfully reduced the number of licensed cars. Another deterrent to owning a car is limited public parking. Meter and on-street parking spaces are scarce; the major parking facilities are multistory car parks where spaces are at a premium. Do not park anywhere unless there is a sign that indicates it is an authorized parking space. If there is no sign, it is considered an illegal spot and you may receive a parking ticket.

By choosing to live in Central, Mid-Levels, or Tsim Sha Tsui, you will find that you can function quite well without a car. However, this lifestyle is best suited to single expatriates or couples. For a family, especially one with school-age children, a car is a necessity if you wish to have some freedom of movement, not only for recreational outings to more remote areas of the New Territories but also for car pooling for after-school events.

Medium- to smaller-sized cars are best suited to Hong Kong, not only because of the narrow, winding, steep roads but also because of the cost of maintenance, gas, and government taxes. For imported cars, new or used, the owner is required to pay a first-registration fee that may range from 70 to 90 percent of the CIF value, that is, the value of the car, insurance, and freight. All cars with steering columns on the left side of the vehicle will have to have them switched, which is not technically advisable. For these reasons, it is usually impractical for most Americans to import a car. Most expatriates therefore buy their cars locally, and many buy used cars. If you are a newcomer and are looking for a car, check local newspapers, supermarket bulletin boards, and other expatriates who are leaving the island and are selling their automobiles. Transfers may be easily arranged by securing the needed forms from the Transportation Department office.

Each year there is an annual auto tax based on the size of the engine and also an additional tax paid to the Traffic Accident Victims Assistance Fund. If you are transferring ownership, be sure that all previous car taxes have been paid since it will be the current owner's responsibility to pay uncollected fees. Third-party insurance is required. Remember when selecting a car that air-conditioning is a necessity in the hot, humid summer months, particularly in Hong Kong's infamous summer traffic jams. Also, have the transmission checked because of the large number of hills to negotiate.

LICENSES

Your national driver's license is sufficient during your first year in Hong Kong. And just as at home, you will be charged a fine by the police if you cannot produce your license upon demand. When applying for a Hong Kong license, in addition to the fee for the license, you will also be levied a fee that is paid to the Traffic Accident Victim's Assistance Fund. If you are a permanent resident of Hong Kong and remaining longer than a year, you will have to obtain a Hong Kong license. As an expatriate, you will not be required to take the customary road test. When applying for a license, bring two passport-sized photos, your passport, and current license. Teenagers under eighteen years of age will be disappointed if they expect to drive in Hong Kong; they cannot drive a car, scooter, or motorcycle. Also, since parents cannot teach their children to drive unless they obtain an instructor's license, you may wish to hire a professional instructor. Invariably, you will easily spot these instructors with their hardworking charges. Their slow-moving vehicles will display a large red *L* on the front and back bumpers as well as the Chinese character for "student."

CAR RENTALS AND HIRES

You may have some occasion to rent a car. If you are a short-term visitor, however, you will probably find it much easier—and less stressful—to use the services of the variety of companies that provide a car and driver.

RULES OF THE ROAD

The Transportation Department provides a small publication called *Highway Code,* which spells out the basic rules. Bicycles are not generally subject to normal traffic rules, and pedestrians have the right-of-way at tram stops and various other places. Your major adjustment will probably be remembering that traffic moves on the left side of the road. Until your response becomes automatic, think twice about which direction to look before you step out into the street. Never stop in any area that has a double yellow line on the curb since it is a restricted area. Areas marked with a single yellow line are restricted only during certain time periods.

11

Leisure Activities

LOCAL RESOURCES, EVENTS, AND FACILITIES

Leisure activities reflect the cultural styles and interests of the Cantonese and the many Western and Asian expatriates who have come to call Hong Kong home. Much of the social life centers around national communities, where a variety of social activities similar to those at home has been organized. The major difference is that at home you know where to find the local theater company, the study group or course, bridge games, and sports facilities. In Hong Kong you must take the initiative to find where these are located. Word of mouth and notices at clubs, shopping centers, and church bulletin boards are the best sources of information. Develop a network of contacts as quickly as you can. Most accompanying spouses have experienced the difficulty of establishing themselves, so make a friend who will introduce you to others of similar backgrounds and interests. The YWCA offers a special program, "At Home in Hong Kong," to welcome newly arrived expatriates.

For persons interested in becoming involved in social service, agencies such as the YWCA, OXFAM, Red Cross, the Marriage and Personal Counseling Service, the Hong Kong Catholic Marriage Advisory Council, Helping Hands, Hong Kong Christian Aid to Refugees, and the Hong Kong Samaritans are interested in adding volunteers and, at times, part-time staff. Consult your consulate, the Hong Kong Council of Social Service, or the Community Advice Bureau as well as the major churches which serve the expatriate community for a current list of social services that offer a useful and rewarding volunteer experience.

CULTURAL ACTIVITIES

Through the efforts of the government, the Urban Council, the Regional Council, and members of the business community, a wide range of cultural events is offered in Hong Kong.

Hong Kong's city hall is rather unique as city halls go, serving not only as a center of government but also as the center of social life. It offers an excellent library, art gallery, museum, concert hall, and rooms for meetings. Various lecture series are held there throughout the year. Because of its location on the harbor, it is also the official greeting place for visiting dignitaries who come to Hong Kong.

The Performing Arts

The Hong Kong Philharmonic Orchestra conducts over 130 concerts a season. Chinese musical interests are represented through the Hong Kong Chinese Orchestra.

Each year there are several cultural festivals which bring world-class performers to Hong Kong. The Festival of Asian Arts is usually held for a period of two and a half weeks in the fall, offering traditional Asian dances, drama, and music. The Hong Kong Arts Festival takes place during the entire month of January and focuses solely on Western music, drama, and dance. The caliber of performance rivals the major cultural centers of the world. Be sure to make your reservations well in advance since this festival is very popular and quickly booked.

The Hong Kong Arts Center, an independent nonprofit organization, provides a wide range of events including music, dance, films, sculpture, and painting. The Center's Schouson Theatre, Recital Hall, and Studio are Hong Kong's centerpiece for encouraging local artists to develop their skills as well as display their works. The center produces *Artslink,* a monthly magazine for members concerning all its activities.

Local neighborhood groups hire Chinese opera troupes for week-long opera celebrations. A bamboo theater is built, usually on the site of the local sports field, to house the performance. Take the time to attend one of these performances in this local setting or at the Koshan Theater, a large open-air theater near Kowloon City. Not only will you gain insight into the nature of Chinese opera, but you will also experience the local residents' appreciation for this art form.

The Hong Kong Dance Company, under the auspices of the Urban Council, features a dance style which draws its inspiration from historical themes and the richness of Chinese dance, expressed in both folk and classical styles. The Modern Dance Theater of Hong Kong is known for its mixture of styles—jazz, modern, and Chinese. The Hong Kong Ballet presents traditional programs.

The Garrison Players and the Hong Kong Stage Club are excellent outlets for amateurs interested in drama. Other professional groups, such as the Chung Ying Theater Company, and amateur groups, such as the Hong Kong Repertory Theater, Asia Theatre, and American Community Theatre (ACT) present Western and Cantonese plays in English and Chinese.

Museums

There are museums and art galleries that display both traditional and contemporary Chinese art. The Hong Kong Museum of Art, housed on two floors of city hall, displays a collection of Chinese art and artifacts, works by local artists, and historical paintings. Ceramics, bronze, lacquer, jade, paintings, and calligraphy are all represented.

The Flagstaff House Museum is housed in a building of historical interest, one of the few remaining colonial structures in Hong Kong. Its specialty is tea ware. The Museum of History in Kowloon Park displays documents related to the evolution of Hong Kong. The Lei Cheung Uk Museum in Kowloon houses a major collection of artifacts from Han

Dynasty excavations. The Space Museum, dedicated to the study of astronomy and space exploration, is located in Kowloon. This museum was the first building of a multiphase project of the Hong Kong Cultural Center, a $77-million-dollar center which opened in November, 1990. It contains three auditoriums, a 2,100-seat emerald-green concert hall in the round, the 1,750-seat crimson Grand Theater, and an informal studio theater as well as restaurants, an expanded Museum of Art, and a garden. The Museum of Science and Technology offers exhibits designed to stimulate an interest in science. Both universities have specialized museums: the Fung Ping Shan Museum, with the world's largest collection of Nestorian Crosses of the Yuan Dynasty as well as other pre-Christian artifacts, and the Art Gallery at the Institute of Chinese Studies of the Chinese University, which exhibits works from Canton. The Museum of Chinese Historical Relics in Wanchai displays many artifacts from China and provides recorded tapes in English and Cantonese to explain the collection. The Hong Kong Railway Museum in the old Tai Po Railway Station highlights the railroad history of a train system that once connected Hong Kong with London. The Police Museum, the reconstructed Wanchai Gap Police Station, records the one hundred and fifty years of service of the Hong Kong Constabulary. Sheung Yiu Folk Museum, Sam Tung Uk Museum, and Tai Fu Tai all provide insights into the folk history of the Chinese landed gentry.

Films

There are over one hundred cinemas in Hong Kong, and approximately one-third of them feature U.S. and British movies with Chinese subtitles. If you are interested in seeing a film, it is best to plan to view it shortly after it is first advertised, since films which do not draw large audiences may be unexpectedly withdrawn. Check the movie guides in the *South China Morning Post* and the *TV and Entertainment Times.* Evening performances are generally at 5:30, 7:30, 9:30, and midnight. Some theaters have afternoon performances at 12:30 and 2:30. One books a seat at a cinema much as one does at the theater, where a particular seat is assigned. Seats can sometimes be reserved in advance and picked up fifteen minutes prior to the performance. It is not uncommon for the Board of Censors or even the theater management to arbitrarily edit American and British films, not only for unacceptable content but also for their length so that all movies fit into the theater's viewing schedules. Hong Kong classifies its films into three categories: Class 1—for all ages, Class 2—parental guidance, and Class 3—eighteen years of age and older. All films in English must have Chinese subtitles, and, likewise, all locally produced Mandarin-language films must have English subtitles.

In addition to the public cinemas, there are private clubs, such as Studio One, which offer films that the public cinemas either cannot or will not run since they do not appeal to the general interests of the community. Membership is not expensive, and it is a worthwhile investment for those who enjoy good European and American films. Alliance Française, the British Council, and the Goethe Institute show French, English, and German films respectively and invite the public to attend. The Film Culture Center of Hong Kong may also be of interest to those who wish to see some original local works.

The Hong Kong International Film Festival takes place during March and April. Contact the Hong Kong Tourist Association for its listing of events and to secure bookings.

Libraries

There are a number of libraries available to expatriates. The major public library system has only a limited collection in English. There are branches at City Hall, Kowloon, North Point, Chai Wan, Lok Fu Sun Chuen, Mong Kok, Quarry Bay, Pok Fulam, Kwun Tong, Wanchai, Kowloon Central, and Aberdeen. The following organizations also have collections open to the public: the Alliance Française Library, the Goethe Institute, the American Library in the United Center in Causeway Bay, the May Institute Library, the YMCA, and the British Council Library. Hong Kong University has a listing of all specialized libraries in the territory and can be helpful in finding needed resources.

COURSES AND HOBBIES

The Chinese University of Hong Kong, the Baptist College, and the University of Hong Kong have departments of extramural studies which offer courses taught in English on a wide range of subjects. Consult the registrar for a current catalogue. Some expatriates have enrolled in undergraduate or graduate programs, especially in Asian Studies. The University of Michigan offers a yearly extension course for a degree in education. Consult your local university for additional educational possibilities. Many organizations provide training programs, lectures, and workshops; and social groups such as the American Women's Association, Island School Evening Institute, and the YWCA offer a variety of lessons, including calligraphy, Japanese flower arranging, Chinese art and cooking, and many others. Consult local newspapers, church bulletins, and supermarket bulletin boards for specific information.

SPORTS

Hong Kong offers an impressive array of sporting activities. In addition to golf, badminton, soccer, ice and roller skating, tennis, and squash, there is every kind of water sport, including good deep-sea fishing. Some people swim at Hong Kong's forty public beaches from mid-March to mid-December although the majority swim only in the warmest months, between June and September. At other times you can have wonderful stretches of beach, like Big Wave Bay or Shek-O Beach, entirely to yourself. The nicest swimming areas are on Sai Kung Peninsula or southern Lantau Island. Many other beaches, unfortunately, are crowded and frequently polluted.

Water-skiers can rent equipment at many marinas along the coast. Skin diving and scuba diving are not very good on the western side of Hong Kong because of sedimentation. The eastern side and the eastern islands of Mirs Bay, the Ninepin Group of islands, and Clearwater Bay are the more preferred areas for diving, but bring your own equipment.

Many expatriates enjoy boating since it provides an opportunity to get away from the crowds, to enjoy the beauty of Hong Kong from the water, and to visit its many outlying islands, some of which are extremely secluded and private. Used boats and junks are frequently listed for sale in the classified ads. The Royal Hong Kong Yacht Club at Kellett Island and the Aberdeen Boat Club on Hong Kong and Hebe Haven in Sai Kung offer moorings and supervision. Contact the Marine Department for information concerning licenses and certificates. Many expatriates purchase part shares in a junk, which takes care of the costs for the mooring facility, the boat boys, and supervision. The Urban Council's Wong Nai Chung Boating Park rents rowing and pedal boats for a pleasant way to enjoy the shoreline of the Southern District of Hong Kong.

Hiking is a popular pastime for Chinese and westerners alike. Country parks stretch for 172 square miles through Hong Kong's countryside, and there are about forty walking and hiking clubs that regularly schedule activities. It is not uncommon to find large groups of Chinese hiking through the New Territories for recreation.

Running has become more of a popular activity. Joggers can be found in Kowloon Park in Tsim Sha Tsui and in Victoria Park on Hong Kong Island. The streets are crowded, so the parks and jogging tracks offer the best opportunity for running. Some adventurous runners jog along the storm drains in the hills above Hong Kong Harbor. The Hong Kong Adventist Hospital offers a running clinic. Or you may be interested in the Hash House Harriers, an international group of men and women who meet to run and then to gather for camaraderie and beverage.

The most popular spectator sport is horse racing, which dates back to Hong Kong's early days. Happy Valley and the Shatin Racecourse offer abundant opportunity for the sporting and gambling interests of Chinese and westerner alike under the watchful eyes of the Royal Hong Kong Jockey Club, a nonprofit organization which donates all its profits to charitable and community projects. Off-track betting centers are located throughout the city.

Hong Kong's International Seven-A-Side Rugby Competition, the Macau Grand Prix, the Hong Kong Tennis Classic, the Hong Kong

International Marathon, the Windsurfing Open Championship, the Lawn Bowls Classic, the Hong Kong International Kart Grand Prix, the China Coast Marathon, and the Hong Kong annual Open Golf Championship all provide high quality entertainment.

CLUBS

There are many sports clubs in Hong Kong but most have long waiting lists. Some clubs also cater to certain national groups and have quotas on foreign nationalities as well as the local Chinese. You may be required to purchase a debenture to secure your membership. In choosing a club, ask your colleagues for their recommendations to help you choose a club that will suit your needs and your personal style. The following is a partial listing of the clubs:

Aberdeen Boat Club
Aberdeen Marina
Clearwater Bay Golf and Country Club
Club de Recreio
Craigengower Cricket Club
Discovery Bay Golf Club
Hebe Haven Yacht Club
Hilltop Country Club
Hong Kong Club
Hong Kong Country Club
Hong Kong Cricket Club
Hong Kong Football Club
Kowloon Cricket Club
Royal Hong Kong Golf Club
Royal Hong Kong Jockey Club
Royal Hong Kong Yacht Club
Shek-O Country Club
South China Athletic Association
United Services Recreation Club
Victoria Recreation Club

YWCA
YMCA

There are all manner of groups for lawyers, nurses, physicians, and other professionals in Hong Kong. In addition, there are special-interest groups such as dinner clubs, bird-watching clubs, camera groups, chess associations, bridge clubs, as well as groups for those interested in cooking, flying, archeology, astronomy, archery, and backgammon. The following is just a partial listing of some of the more well-known clubs. Consult the English Yellow Pages or the Community Advice Bureau for information on these and other groups, including a large number of national associations.

American Club
American Country Club
American Women's Association
Catholic Club
Dynasty Club
Foreign Correspondents' Club
Hong Kong Association of Business and Professional Women
Hong Kong Association of University Women
Hong Kong Club
Hong Kong Council of Women
Hong Kong Women's International Club
Indian Recreation Club
Jewish Recreation Club
Kowloon Club
Ladies Recreation Club
Lions Club
Rotary Club of Hong Kong
Rotary Club of Kowloon
Soroptimist Club of Hong Kong
U.S. League of Women Voters
Women's Corona Society
Zonta Clubs of Hong Kong

The Hong Kong Convention and Incentive Travel Bureau publishes a yearly listing entitled "Associations and Societies in Hong Kong," detailing the names, addresses, and leadership of all representative associations and societies in Hong Kong. Its topical index is extremely useful for identifying resources.

RELIGIOUS AFFILIATION

Most faiths and denominations are represented in Hong Kong and offer services in English. Included in their number are Anglicans, Roman Catholics, Baptists, Quakers, Lutherans, Methodists, Presbyterians, Christian Scientists, Mormons, Seventh-Day Adventists, Jews, and Muslims. Consult the Saturday edition of the *South China Morning Post* for the most current list of times of services, addresses, and telephone numbers.

CHINESE FESTIVALS

For the adventurous expatriate, the cycle of Chinese festivals provides not only recreation but also a way of entering the culture. The key to enjoying the holidays is to find a Chinese colleague or acquaintance who can be a guide. Not only are they wonderful outings which will deepen your understanding of Chinese culture, but they are also an enjoyable and memorable experience.

Contemporary festivals are based on the mythical and historical events of Chinese tradition. Most festivals center on family and food, and involve boisterous celebration.

The first is *Chinese New Year*. This traditional celebration varies year by year since the holiday is set on the lunar calendar. The holiday usually occurs during the last weeks of January or the beginning weeks of February and lasts fifteen days, although the official public celebration is only three days. Families customarily gather on the eve of Chinese New Year for a meal. Many of the courses have a special meaning, such as the fish dish, which signifies hope for abundance during the coming year (the words for "fish" and "abundance" have the same sound but a different tone). Following the meal, families visit the flower markets at Choi Hung Cheun in Kowloon and Victoria Park in Causeway Bay to purchase red flowers, small mandarin orange trees, narcissus, and peach and plum blossoms to decorate their homes. The end of the New Year celebration is the *Yuen Siu Festival,* when colorful lanterns are prepared and displayed in homes, public places, temples, and central halls.

You may wish to have a special staff banquet for New Year, and you will definitely be giving out many gifts of money. Be prepared to give your Chinese house staff an extra month's salary at this time. If you are married, give children and young unmarried Chinese friends red envelopes containing small amounts of money (*lai see* packets). (If you are not married, you don't need to give anything.) Customarily, you include one or two Hong Kong ten-dollar bills for close friends and only a few dollars for children. If you forget to distribute lai see at New Year's, the children delight in reminding you. In addition, you should give a packet to each member of your household staff, service providers, and office subordinates. This latter group receives more sizeable packets. Consult a trusted office colleague or a long-term expatriate for advice on the exact amount. Remember, always place an even amount of money in the packets.

Learn a few of the Chinese greetings during this season. The most common is *Kung hay fat choi,* which means "May you have wealth and good fortune." If you are affiliated with personnel from the People's Republic of China, the Chinese New Year's celebration we are referring to is called the *Spring Festival* or *Chung Chieu.* The PRC follows the Gregorian, or solar, calendar and celebrates the New Year on January 1. Chung Chieu is celebrated in the PRC, although many of the traditional New Year's customs are discouraged by the government because they are believed to be superstitious.

Many expatriates feel a little out of step in Hong Kong at New Year's since business comes to a complete stop. All Chinese are involved with their families and there is an atmosphere of celebration which is foreign to expatriates at this time of the year. You might enjoy testing your own skills at Chinese cooking (which will be necessary anyway if your Chinese staff are at their own home celebrating) by inviting your closest friends for a dinner on New Year's Eve. Be sure to stock up on your food supply well in advance since stores will not only be closed on New Year's Day but on the following two or three days as well. Stores will be crowded prior to New Year since it is the custom to buy new clothes and to get a haircut. Many expatriates, as well as the wealthier Chinese, like to travel during this vacation week. If you choose to do so, book your reservations well in advance.

During the months of March, April and May, Hong Kong celebrates the *Ching Ming Festival,* the *birthday of Tin Hau,* the *birthday of Buddha,* and the *Cheung Chau Bun Festival.* These relatively localized celebrations are fun to observe. Ching Ming Festival is a time when families visit ancestors' graves. One way of respectfully observing this ritualized holiday is to visit the Ching Chung Koon Taoist Temple or the Castle Peak Monastery (both located in the New Territories), to observe both the Taoist and Buddhist rites for the dead.

On the birthday of Tin Hau, goddess of fishermen, attempt to borrow someone's junk and sail to Joss House Bay for the ceremonial worship of the goddess or visit the Taoist temple in Stanley.

To celebrate the birthday of the Lord Buddha, plan to travel either to the Po Lin Monastery on Lantau Island, where you will be able to see the world's largest outdoor Buddha cast in bronze and weighing 250 tons, or to the Temple of the 10,000 Buddhas monastery in Shatin to observe the Buddha-Bathing Ceremony.

The Cheung Chau Bun Festival, or Tai Chui, takes place on Cheung Chau Island. Its purpose is to appease the spirits that create storms and illness. For several days people engage in rituals directed at assuring their protection from the spirits. Three large towers of bread in the form of stacked buns are built to feed the hungry spirits. It is considered good luck to take one of the buns home. In addition to the rituals conducted at the Pak Tai Temple, there are parades, floats, music, and Chinese opera.

Some time in June is *Tuen Ng Festival,* popularly known as the Dragon Boat Festival. It celebrates the death of Ch'u Yuen, who was drowned at sea and whose boatmen raced to reach his body in the water before the sharks did. Throughout Hong Kong, teams enter competitive races which have now gained international status. The expatriate version of this competition takes place at Stanley Beach. It's a good day for a picnic. The next notable celebration is the *Mid-Autumn Festival,* or "Mooncake" Festival, a family event for which children make lanterns and walk at night around the neighborhoods. And when you look at the moon in Hong Kong, don't bother to look for the "Man in the Moon" on the moon's surface. You are supposed to see a rabbit instead and the beautiful lady who lives with him. Actually the celebration recalls an uprising of the Han people against the Mongolians in fourteenth-century China, when plans for a revolution were concealed within cakes. Be sure to have your children make lanterns to take with them to Victoria Peak or any of the open parks or beaches to see families enjoying this holiday and to participate yourselves.

There are two additional celebrations which reflect the Chinese respect for their ancestors: *Chung Yeung,* celebrated in October, and *Yue Lan,* celebrated in August. Chung Yeung commemorates the manner in which a Han Dynasty man protected his family from an unexpected flood and illness by following the advice of a sage to retreat to a mountaintop. Join the local people and hike in Hong Kong's rural parks in the New Territories and have a picnic. During Yue Lan you will find many people burning offerings of paper money and paper constructions of food, houses, and cars as offerings to spirits of the dead who supposedly roam the world on that evening.

EXCURSIONS

Areas in and around Hong Kong

Hong Kong may be small, but it is varied and interesting. An eight-minute tram ride to the top of Victoria Peak (1,911 feet) gives one a bird's-eye view of the active harbor, high-rise skyline, and planes flying in and out of Kai Tak Airport. Following refreshments in the terminal at the Peak Tower, enjoy the city's panorama and a fine nature walk around the Peak.

Aberdeen Harbor truly reflects the complexity and contrasts of Hong Kong. In one direction, you see the activity of some twenty thousand fishermen and -women who live and work on their junks, sampans, and seagoing trawlers. Here floating restaurants and shop-keepers move about, servicing this water-based community. In the opposite direction, you find the vast collection of yachts and pleasure junks of the expatriates and wealthy Chinese, the contrast highlighting the extremes that exist side by side in Hong Kong. You can hire a sampan to ferry you about the harbor.

The Central District can best be explored in the byways near the Western Market. There you will find a maze of narrow streets jammed with vendors, bargain stalls, small shops, and a profusion of Chinese banners and slim vertical signs proclaiming the multitude of wares for sale. By walking around the district, you will be able to see what the local Chinese purchase for their own homes. Stop at the stores where wooden barrels are heaped with rice and a variety of dried products. Enter an herbal medicine shop and, if possible, strike up a conversation with the proprietor. Visit Wing Sing Street, known as Egg Street because any kind of egg, including the one-hundred-year-old variety, can be purchased there. The specialty of Wing Lok Street is Chinese *chops,* a carved stone used as a seal (a kind of personal signature). Take plenty of time to walk the streets, enter the stores, and ask questions.

Kowloon Peninsula is best known for its hotels, its nightlife, and its hostess clubs. Eventually the complex surrounding the Space Museum will change the character of this section of town into a cultural center much as the major shopping centers of Tsim Sha Tsui East have raised the quality of shopping in old Tsim Sha Tsui. A walk down Nathan Road for approximately one and one-half miles will place you in one of the major non-Western shopping areas of Hong Kong. On the way, stop at the Islamic Center for an introduction to the history of the Muslim community in Hong Kong. The park next to it is a wonderful place to observe the elderly of Hong Kong performing their *tai'chi.* Here, particularly in the morning and evening, you will often see men carrying bird cages and walking their birds, both pets and owners enjoying a bit of morning or evening fresh air.

Tucked deep within Kowloon but easily accessible by the MTR is Wong Tai Sin Temple, considered by many to be the most popular and lucky of all Hong Kong temples. The visitor has an opportunity to see the popular expression of religious sentiment and to examine the many stalls of fortune-tellers who divine people's future through a variety of obscure means. Don't be offended by the number of people begging at the entrance of the temple since offering alms to the needy when one visits a temple is a pious gesture as well as a guarantee of good fortune.

On the south coast near Aberdeen is Ocean Park, one of the world's most outstanding ocean museums. Here you can walk along an underwater reef gallery and see some five hundred species of fish in their natural habitat and watch the performances of porpoises and killer whales at the Ocean Theater. The 170-acre park boasts one of the longest outdoor escalators, a dramatic roller coaster, a zoo, a cable car system, and a walk-through aviary. Water World, occupying the adjacent sixty-five acres, offers a variety of swimming pools and water slides. A special section, Adventure World, with its animals and play area, is especially suitable for children. The Middle Kingdom recreates five thousand years of Chinese history by presenting the sights, sounds, and encounters of thirteen different Chinese dynasties. A special treat is the Chinese restaurant which serves food from all the provinces of China. An open-air theater provides lion dancers, magicians, and acrobats.

Sung Dynasty Village takes you back in time to a typical Chinese township of the Sung Dynasty period (A.D. 960-1279). All employees are in period dress, and they provide demonstrations of the martial arts, magic, calligraphy, and traditional ceremonies such as the wedding service. A visit is not only an introduction to Chinese cultural heritage; it also helps sharpen one's eye as to how these traditions are still being followed in Hong Kong. Nearby, in Laichikok, is the Laichikok Amusement Park offering a variety of carnival rides as well as performances of Chinese opera.

The New Territories is no longer solely a glimpse into rural China. The Hakka villages still exist, such as that at Kam Tin Walled Village constructed in the 1600s, and the architectural buff can find many ancestral buildings to study. And Sam Tung Uk Museum in Tsuen Wan and Sheun Yiu in Sai Kung are noteworthy. But, the New Territories has also become a modern extension of Hong Kong with many New Towns dotting its open spaces.

Ching Chung Koon, the Temple of Green Pines, is famous for its devotion to prayers for Hong Kong's deceased. It offers the visitor an excellent opportunity to observe Taoist ritual prayers for the dead, especially during the New Year's celebration. It also displays an extensive collection of Chinese dwarf trees. You may wish to stop at the Miu Fat Monastery for a vegetarian lunch. Other monasteries of note in the New Territories are the Chuk Lam Sim Yuen (Bamboo Forest Monastery) above Tsuen Wan, the Castle Peak Monastery near Castle Peak, and the Temple of the 10,000 Buddhas, reached by climbing 431 steps cut into the hills above Shatin. Each of these monasteries gives a different insight into the religious underpinnings of Chinese society and therefore provides an opportunity not only for exploration but also for learning about the culture. And of course, by touring the rural areas of the New Territories, you will be able to glimpse Chinese duck or fish farms.

In Lam Tseun Valley, the Kadoorie Experimental and Extension Farm and Botanical Gardens, with its terraced orchards and hillsides, provides a pleasant and quiet diversion to the pace of the city. Entry is free, but reservations are required at least two days in advance.

The Shatin area has become quite developed mainly because of the presence of the Shatin Racecourse, where races are held from September to May. The Happy Dragon Recreation Park provides an amusement center as well as an aquatic world, and next door is a bicycle park.

The Outlying Islands of Hong Kong

There are many publications that outline in detail the beauty and interest of Hong Kong's outlying islands, so we will offer only a thumbnail sketch here. By boarding a ferry or sharing a junk, you can quickly leave behind the chaotic pace of Hong Kong and enjoy the contrasting peace of the islands, each of which has a character of its own.

Twice the size of Hong Kong, Lantau is easily accessible via inexpensive ferry service on both its east and west coasts. Many ferries make the crossing daily from the Outer Island Ferry terminal a half mile from the Star Ferry. Lantau has experienced extensive development during the 1980s—the planned residential community at Discovery Bay, a modern golf course, and the Sea Ranch Resort Club. In the 1990s the Hong Kong government will be building a new airport at Chek Lap Kok on the north side of Lantau Island, which is scheduled to replace Kai Tak Airport. One runway is scheduled to be operational by 1997. Lantau continues to be home to many monks and nuns who have established their monasteries within its quiet hills and mountains. Po Lin Monastery is the most prestigious Buddhist center in Hong Kong and provides overnight accommodations, Buddhist-style, for the adventurous expatriate. It has an excellent vegetarian meal service. By staying here or at the Lantau Tea Gardens at Ngong Ping nearby, one can walk to Fung Wong Sham (Sunset Peak), Lantau's high peak, for the sunrise. The Trappist Haven Monastery of Our Lady of Liesse provides overnight accommodations for retreat groups and visitors. If the religious tone of Lantau is too restricting for your taste, the Silvermine Beach Hotel, with beaches nearby as well as the Silvermine Restaurant offer secular alternatives. Other noteworthy destinations are the cities of Tai-O and Tung Chung, both ports that have histories dating back two hundred years. In Tung Chung the early Sung Dynasty Court of China took refuge when driven out by the Mongols. The old fort there was later equipped with Chinese and European cannons for use against opium runners.

Lamma Island is a frequent refuge for expatriates who own junks, since it is relatively close to the moorings of Aberdeen. Third largest of all the Hong Kong islands, it maintains a predominantly agricultural tone. Its two ports, Kok Kwu Wan at Picnic Bay and Yung Shue Wan, have many fine restaurants. Lamma's uniqueness lies in its wonderful walking trails, secluded beaches, and the opportunity it offers to enjoy the out-of-doors.

Peng Chau and Cheung Chau islands are primarily fishing villages. As your ferry from Central enters Cheung Chau Harbor, you will see the industrial and family fishing boats dotting the harbor and the holding pens used for their catches. The pace of the island is peaceful, its life centering around the sea. It is known for its shipbuilding, its restaurants, and its festivals honoring the gods Kwun Yum and Pak Tai. No cars are permitted on the island. The Bun Festival surrounding the

Pak Tin Temple draws many visitors. Another attraction is the Cave of Cheung Po Chai, which only the small of girth dare to pass through. There are a number of beaches on the island, Tung Wan Beach being the most popular. A variety of restaurants serving Western and Cantonese food is available as well as one of Hong Kong's few "out-of-town" hotels, the Warwick.

Peng Chau is the smallest of all the islands and retains its fishing-village character. If visitors enjoy the tone of this island, they may also enjoy the adventure of visiting many of the other small islands surrounding Hong Kong. Visiting these places gives the expatriate some insight into the life of the coastal Chinese. Some of the more interesting islands are Kat O Chau, Ap Chau and Po Toi. Two areas are off limits: Sek Kwu Chau, a residential treatment center for drug addicts, and Sunshine Island, the former leper colony which is currently used as a temporary camp for boat people awaiting transfer to other countries or repatriation to Vietnam.

Excursions into the People's Republic of China

Travel into China is convenient for people living in Hong Kong. Use local Hong Kong travel agents to select a one-day trip or a more comprehensive tour of China. If you are adventurous, you can arrange your own trips, either a day's visit to Shenzhen or to Zhongshan, the birthplace of Dr. Sun Yat-sen, or a "getaway" weekend in Guangzhou. Be sure to secure a visa to travel in China should you plan to be your own tour director or the tour director for your friends and family.

Excursion to Macau

Macau was one of the early outposts of European commercial expansion in Asia, its colonization preceding that of Hong Kong. The Portuguese have maintained their colony in Macau since 1557. Consisting of two islands, Taipei and Coloane, and the Macau peninsula extending from the district of Foshan, this 16.92 square-kilometer (6.53 square-mile) colony has a population of approximately 450,000 people. Considered a Chinese territory under Portuguese administration, Macau has lived a very tentative existence, attempting to balance the interests of Portugal and China. Macau will become a Special Administrative Region of the People's Republic of China on December 20, 1999.

Macau makes a wonderful one- or two-day trip. The pace and life-style is more relaxed than that of hectic and congested Hong Kong, the architectural design reminiscent of older colonial days and of Europe. Enjoying the cobblestone streets, tree-lined boulevards, and pastel-colored villas, you will feel yourself unwind and relax. There are quality hotels and restaurants as well as reasonable Portuguese wine. Macau is so small you may easily walk through it, or if need be you can hire a pedicab, taxi, or small self-drive vehicle called a *minimoke.* Macau is famous for its gambling, its major casinos very popular among Hong Kong gamblers.

Traveling to Macau is relatively easy via ferry, jetfoil, hover-ferry, jetcat, or Hydrofoil. Before leaving Hong Kong, buy a round-trip ticket, especially for weekends and holidays, since it is extremely difficult to get return bookings without reservations. You must bring your passport, but if you are a United States or British citizen, you will not need to obtain a visa for Macau.

CHILDREN AND YOUTH

For children accustomed to living in suburbs or less populated environments, the major challenge of living in Hong Kong is becoming adjusted to a metropolitan life-style and learning the skills of urban living. After a short period of adjustment, however, children find Hong Kong an interesting and exciting place (see "Activities" below). Parents quickly discover that it is a safe city and easy for their children to negotiate because of the comprehensive transportation system.

Baby-sitting

Many expatriates use their household staff or hire amahs to help with child care and baby-sitting. If you need to travel out of Hong Kong, however, you may not feel comfortable leaving your children under the total supervision of the amah. Most parents solve this dilemma by asking a neighbor or friend to check in on the children and the amah frequently. The only registered group that provides baby-sitters is an organization called Rent-a-Mom. You can also contact the Community Advice Bureau for help in finding expatriate children who wish to baby-sit.

Work Opportunities

Hong Kong is a difficult place for young people to find a job. One source of help is the American Chamber of Commerce, which has a summer job program for young people that ranges from volunteer social service to clerical positions.

Activities

Young people will find that Hong Kong offers a large number of activities. First, there is the sea and all the water sports. Most teens network through their school friends to find a family or corporate junk to enjoy together on the ocean. Many of the clubs mentioned earlier become the centers of sporting and social activities oriented around club tennis matches, swimming facilities, or just a delicious hamburger to be enjoyed with friends at the downtown club after school. Visits to the Sung Dynasty Village, a replica of a Sung village; the Lai Chi Kok Amusement Park; and Ocean Park are also interesting.

Hong Kong is not a community where children ride bicycles extensively. You will see adults riding racing bicycles and, unfortunately, causing congestion, especially on the narrow roads of Hong Kong Island. There are, however, several safe places for children as well as adults to enjoy bicycle riding: the Shatin Bicycle Garden in Shatin, the Taimeitak Center in Taipo, and the beach areas of Silvermine Bay.

Other activities of interest to children are Little League baseball and the scouting programs associated with the Hong Kong Girl Guides Association, Girl's Brigade, Hong Kong Council of the Boy's Brigade, and the Scouts Association of Hong Kong. Consult your child's school for the nearest program. For chess fans there is the annual Student's Championships in August. The American Club offers a twelve-session, two-dinner ballroom dance series for ages eleven to eighteen. Also look for notices of gymnastics and martial arts courses and competitions. They are excellent skill-building activities for children.

The Hong Kong Outward Bound School maintains two residential bases—one in Tai Mong Tsai, Sai Kung, and the other in Mirs Bay. In addition they offer a twin-masted ship, the Ji Fung (or Spirit of Resolution) for sea-based training programs. Activities are offered in the summer for children. The YMCA, the Hong Kong International School, and other educational institutions offer recreational and academic programs during the summer months.

ENJOYING HONG KONG AND ITS CULTURE

The final chapters of this book list a number of sources and reading materials for additional information. Learning about a new place—reading its history, exploring its customs and traditions, and getting acquainted with its people—contributes to enjoying and becoming part of it. Most expatriates find Hong Kong and the Chinese intriguing and engaging. This volume provides only the first step of this journey.

12

Sources of Information

In the United States

For information on Hong Kong/American Government trading:

British Embassy
Office of the Commissioner for
  Hong Kong Commercial Affairs
680 5th Avenue
22nd Floor
New York, NY 10019
212-265-8888

Hong Kong Economic and Trade Office
1233 20th Street NW
Washington, DC 20036
202-331-8947

Hong Kong Economic and Trade Office
180 Sutter Street
San Francisco, CA 94104
415-677-9038

For political and economic policy information:

Office of Chinese and Mongolian Affairs
EAP Room 4318
U.S. State Department
Washington, DC 20520
202-647-9141

U.S. Information Agency
Hong Kong Desk
301 4th Street SW
Washington, DC 20547
202-619-4700

For information on Hong Kong business regulations, rental space, warehousing:

Hong Kong Industrial Promotion Office
680 5th Avenue
22nd Floor
New York, NY 10019
212-265-7232

For information on commercial issues, marketing information, lists of Hong Kong manufacturers and business organizations:

United States Commerce Department
Hong Kong Desk Officer
ITA/Office of China and Hong Kong
Room 2317
14th Street and Constitution Avenue NW
Washington, DC 20230
202-377-3583

U.S. Department of Labor
Bureau of Labor Statistics
200 Constitution Avenue NW
Washington, DC 20212
202-523-6043 (Hong Kong desk)

Hong Kong Trade Development Council
673 5th Avenue, 4th Floor
New York, NY 10022
212-838-8688
fax: 212-838 8941

Consult your local directory for T.D.C. offices in Dallas, Los Angeles, Chicago, Miami, and Vancouver.

For monetary information:

U.S. Department of Treasury
Hong Kong Desk
Office of International Monetary Affairs
15th Street and Pennsylvania Avenue NW
Washington, DC 20220
202-566-2011

For agricultural information:

U.S. Department of Agriculture
Foreign Agriculture Services
Independence Avenue at 12th and 14th Streets SW
Washington, DC 20250
202-447-3935

For free information guides to the Hong Kong tax system:

Touche Ross International
PO Box 778

Radio City Station
1633 Broadway
New York, NY 10019
212-489-1600

Price Waterhouse
1251 Avenue of the Americas
New York, NY 10020
212-489-8900

For customs information:

U.S. Customs Department
1301 Constitution Avenue NW
Washington, DC 20229
202-566-8195

For visa information:

British Embassy
Office of the Counselor for
  Hong Kong Commercial Affairs
3100 Massachusetts Avenue NW
Washington, DC 20008
202-462-1340

For health information:

Superintendent of Documents
U.S. Government Printing Office
Washington, DC 20402
202-783-3238

For $5.00 you can purchase a copy of "Health Information for International Travel," a comprehensive handbook updated yearly.

Maryland Center for Disease Control Hot Line
404-332-4559

For infomation on studying in Hong Kong:

Institute of International Education
809 United Nations Plaza
New York, NY 10017
212-883-8200

Council on International Educational Exchange
205 East 42nd Street
New York, NY 10017
212-661-1414

International Schools Services, Inc.
15 Roszel Road
Princeton, NJ 08540
609-452-0990

For general tourist information:

Hong Kong Tourist Association
590 5th Avenue
New York, NY 10036
212-869-5008

Request a Tourist Information Kit, free of charge, which contains
general information on Hong Kong business, culture, food, geog-
raphy, history, and culture. Consult your local directory for H.K.T.A.
offices in Chicago, Los Angeles, San Francisco, and Toronto.

In Hong Kong

For governmental information:

American Consulate General
Commercial Section
17th Floor
26 Garden Road
St. John's Building, H.K.
852-5211467
fax: 852-8459800

For business information:

American Chamber of Commerce in Hong Kong
Room 1030
10th Floor Swire House
Charter Road
Central, H.K.
852-5260165
fax: 852-8101289

Provides information on advertising, business briefings, access to business directories and references, Chinese trade information, and community service projects.

Hong Kong General Chamber of Commerce
United Centre
22nd Floor
95 Queensway
G.P.O. Box 852, H.K.
852-5299229
fax: 852-5279843

Chinese General Chamber of Commerce
7th Floor
24-25 Connaught Road
Central, H.K.
852-5256385
fax: 852-8452610

Hong Kong Productivity Council
World Commerce Center
12th Floor
Harbour City
11 Canton Road
Kowloon, H.K.
852-7351656
fax: 852-7357229

Business Registration Office
Inland Revenue Department
Windsor House 3/F
311 Gloucester Road
Causeway Bay, H.K.
852-8943149
fax: 852-5766359

Hong Kong Trade Development Office
Hong Kong Convention and Exhibition Center
37th Floor
Office Tower
1 Harbour Road
Wanchai, H.K.
852-8334333
fax: 852-8240249

For residential information:

Hong Kong Immigration Department
Wanchai II
7 Gloucester Road
Wanchai, H.K.
8256111

Hong Kong Tourist Association
35th Floor
Jardine House
1 Connaught Place
Central, H.K.
852-8017111
fax: 852-8104877

13

Recommended Reading

Culture

Ancestral Images. Dr. Hugh Baker. Hong Kong: *S.C.M. Post*, 1979.

Beyond the Chinese Face. Michael Harris Bond. Hong Kong: Oxford University Press, 1991.

The Book of Chinese Beliefs. Frena Bloomfield. New York: Ballantine, 1989.

Chinese Creeds and Customs. V. R. Burkhard. Hong Kong: *S.C.M. Post*, 1953, 1955, 1958.

Chinese Culture in Hong Kong. S. Y. Ng and Shirley C. Ingram. Hong Kong: Asia 2000, 1989.

The Ethos of the Hong Kong Chinese. Lau Siu Kai and Kuan Hsi Chi. Hong Kong: Chinese University-Cornet Books, 1989.

Fragrant Harbour. John Warner. Hong Kong: John Warner Publications, 1986.

History of Hong Kong. G. B. Endacott. Hong Kong: Oxford University Press, 1973.

Hong Kong: The Colony That Never Was. Alan Birch. Hong Kong: Twin Age, 1991.

Lectures on Hong Kong History. K. C. Fok. Hong Kong: Commercial Press, 1990.

The Occult World of Hong Kong. Frena Bloomfield. Hong Kong: Hong Kong Publishing Co., 1980.

The Psychology of the Chinese People. Michael Harris Bond. Hong Kong: Oxford University Press, 1986.

Social Issues in Hong Kong. Benjamin K. Leung. London: Oxford University Press, 1990.

Temples. Joyce Savidge. Hong Kong: Government Information Services, 1977.

Business and Economy

The Asia Business Book. David Rearwin. Yarmouth, ME: Intercultural Press, 1991.

The Banking System of Hong Kong. T. K. Ghose. Singapore: Butterworth, 1987.

Chinese Commercial Negotiating Style. Lucien W. Pye. Cambridge, MA: Oelgeschlager, Gunn and Hain, 1982.

Directory of American Business in Hong Kong. Hong Kong: GTE Directories, 1991.

Doing Business in Today's Hong Kong. American Chamber of Commerce in Hong Kong. London/New York: Oxford University Press, 1988.

The Economic Future of Hong Kong. Miron Hushkat. Boulder, CO: Lynne Rienner, 1990.

"Establishing an Office in Hong Kong." American Chamber of Commerce in Hong Kong. Hong Kong: American Chamber of Commerce, 1991.

Going International: How to Make Friends and Deal Effectively in the Global Marketplace. Lennie Copeland and Lewis Griggs. New York: New American Library Penguin, 1986.

Hong Kong for the Business Visitor. Hong Kong: Hong Kong Trade Development Council. (Published in seven languages: English, French, German, Italian, Spanish, Japanese, and Chinese.)

Hong Kong Marketing Management at the Crossroads. C. F. Yang, S. C. Ho, and H. M. Yau. Hong Kong: The Commercial Press, 1989.

Industrial Relations and Law in Hong Kong. Joseph England. Hong Kong: Oxford University Press, 1989.

Management Case Studies in Hong Kong. Sara F. Y. Tang and Alma M. Whiteley. Hong Kong: Longman Group (Far East), 1991.

Managing Cultural Differences. Phillip R. Harris and Robert T. Moran. Houston: Gulf Publishing Co., 1987.

The New China: Comparative Economic Development in Mainland China, Taiwan and Hong Kong. Alvin Rabushka. Boulder, CO: Westview Press, 1987.

The Spirit of Chinese Capitalism. S. Gordon Redding. New York: de Gruyter, 1990.

Reference

Asia Yearbook. Hong Kong: *Far Eastern Economic Review.* Yearly.

Background Notes on Hong Kong. The State Department. (To order, write to: Superintendent of Documents, U.S. Government Printing Office, Washington, DC 20402-9325 or call 202-783-3238.)

Children's Guide to Hong Kong. Ellen O'Connor. Hong Kong: *S.C.M. Post,* 1981.

Hong Kong: Great Cities of the World. Frank Fischbeck. Hong Kong: Formasia, 1986. (photography)

Hong Kong. Hong Kong: Hong Kong Government. Annual official yearbook.

The Hong Kong Baby Book. Julie Blatter Pierce, ed. Hong Kong: Corporate Communications, 1990.

The Huppy Handbook—Life and Times of the Young Hong Kong Professional. Hong Kong: Pose, 1988.

Insight Guides: Hong Kong. Singapore: APA Productions, 1986.

Let's Go to Hong Kong. Keith Lye. Hong Kong: Franklin Watts, 1983. (A book directed to children.)

Living in Hong Kong. Hong Kong: Amcham Publications, 1988.

Setting Up in Hong Kong. Fiona Campbell. Hong Kong: F.D.C. Services, 1990.

Survival Kit for Overseas Living. L. Robert Kohls. Yarmouth, ME: Intercultural Press, Inc., 1984.

Government and Politics

City on the Rocks: Hong Kong's Uncertain Future. Kevin Rafferty. New York: Viking Books, 1990.

The Government and Politics of Hong Kong. N. J. Miners. London: Oxford University Press, 1986.

Hong Kong. Jan Morris. New York: Random House, 1988.

Hong Kong 1997—The Final Settlement. David Bonavia. Bromely, London: Columbus Books, 1985.

Hong Kong, A Chinese and International Concern. Edited by Jugen Doman and Yu-Ming Shaw. London: Westview Press, 1988.

Hong Kong: A Study in Bureaucracy and Politics. P. Harris. Hong Kong: Macmillan, 1985.

Hong Kong and 1997: Strategies for the Future. Edited by Y. C. Jao, Leung Chi Keung, P. Wesley-Smith, and Wong Siu Lun. Hong Kong: University of Hong Kong, 1985.

The Other Hong Kong Report. Y. C. Wong and Y. S. Cheng. Hong Kong: Chinese University, 1990.

A People Misruled: Hong Kong and the Chinese Stepping-Stone Syndrome. Albert H. Yee. Hong Kong: API Press, 1990.

Quick Tidings of Hong Kong. Austin Coates. London: Oxford University Press, 1990.

Society and Politics in Hong Kong. Lau Siu Kai. New York: Coronet Publishing, 1982.

Unequal Treaty—1898-1997. Peter Wesley-Smith. Hong Kong: Oxford University Press, 1984.

Leisure

Drummond's Hong Kong Guide to Art and Antique Dealers. Hong Kong: Drummond's, 1986.

Hong Kong Best Restaurants. Hong Kong: *Hong Kong Tattler,* 1992.

Hong Kong Factory Bargains. Dana Goetz. Hong Kong: Delta Dragon Publications, 1990.

Hong Kong Gems and Jewelry. Joan Reid Ahreni and Ruth Lor Malloy. Hong Kong: Delta Dragon Publications, 1986.

Hong Kong Guide Maps. Hong Kong: Universal Publications, 1987.

Hong Kong Heritage—Historical Buildings and Antiquities in Hong Kong. Hong Kong: Government Information Services, 1989.

Hong Kong Shopping Guide. Barbara Anderson-Tsang and Leopoldine Mikula. Hong Kong: Professional Presenters, 1991.

Hong Kong—Yin and Yang. Dana Goetz. Hong Kong: Delta Dragon Publications, 1990.

In Search of the Past: A Guide to the Antiquities of Hong Kong. Soloman Bard. Hong Kong: URBCO, 1988.

Time Out Collection. Bary Girling. Hong Kong: TV and Entertainment Times, 1990.

Twelve Hong Kong Walks. Derek Kemp. Hong Kong: Oxford University Press, 1985.

Literature

Dynasty. Robert Elegant. New York: McGraw-Hill, 1977; and Glasgow: William Collins and Sons, 1977.

The Honourable Schoolboy. John Le Carré. London: Hodder and Stoughton, 1977.

Noble House. James Clavell. New York: Dell Publishing Company, 1981; and London: Hodder and Stoughton, 1981.

Tai-Pan. James Clavel. New York: Atheneum and Dell, 1966.

Periodicals

The Asian Manager (quarterly). Asian Institute of Management. AIM, 123 Paseo de Roxas, Makati, M. M., Philippines. Tel: (632) 874011.

Hong Kong Economic Journal (daily). Fourth Floor, Block A, North Point Industrial Building, 499 King's Road. Tel: 5626221.

Hong Kong Economic Times (daily). Third Floor, Cheong Kong Building, 661 King's Road. Tel: 5651833.

Hong Kong, Inc. (monthly). Capital Communications Corporation, Twenty-fourth Floor, Westlands Center, 20 Westlands Road, Quarry Bay, Hong Kong. Tel: 8112006.

Hong Kong Trader (monthly). Thirty-first Floor, Great Eagle Centre, 23 Harbour Road. Tel: 8334333. Telex: 73595.

South China Morning Post (daily). Tong Chong Street, P.O. Box 47. Tel: 5652222. Telex: 86008.